Daily Buddhist Practice Guide

How to Practice Buddhism
at Home and in Everyday Life

By Alan Peto

First Edition September 2022
Published by Alan Peto

ISBN: 978-1-7354003-3-4 (Paperback)
ISBN: 978-1-7354003-4-1 (eBook)

*This book is dedicated to all sentient beings
who have found the Buddha's Dharma
and aspire to be freed from suffering.*

Table of Contents

Welcome!

Congratulations! By reading this book, you are taking the first step in joining the half billion Buddhist laypersons[1] around the world who *practice* the religion daily.

But how do you *start* practicing Buddhism?

If you are not yet in a Buddhist tradition[2], trying to "figure out" a daily Buddhist practice on your own can be confusing.

This confusion often exists because Buddhist practices are as diverse as the many different traditions in Buddhism.

And if you are living in a country that is not predominantly Buddhist, there may not be a temple and monastics nearby to help you with learning how to practice.

---

[1] Laypersons are everyday practitioners but are not ordained Buddhist monks or nuns.

[2] Also called "schools", there are different traditions such as Zen and Theravada.

As a Buddhist layperson like yourself, I remember the challenges of trying to practice Buddhism when there was no temple near me.

While you should endeavor to find a Buddhist temple and Buddhist monastics to properly show you how to practice in their tradition, this may not always be possible.

That is why I created this book as a practical guide to help introduce you to Buddhist practice until you find a Buddhist tradition you want to join.

Inside this book you will find guidance on starting your journey into Buddhism by constructing a daily Buddhist practice.

While these various practices may look new and unusual to you, please keep an open mind to them. They are typically the product of centuries of refinement which provide skillful ways of helping us to realizing the Buddhist path of cultivating wisdom, transforming our morality and conduct, and deepening our concentration.

Why is all this important? Because Buddhist practices are designed to help you eventually realize your true natural mental state known as *"Nirvāṇa"* which is free of the "fuel" of suffering and unskillful actions: greed, anger, and ignorance.

Welcome to Buddhism and Buddhist practice! May your journey be an enlightening one.

Why Should I Practice?

For someone who is new to Buddhism, understanding why someone practices every day is important.

Without understanding what motivates someone to practice Buddhism, you may start your journey on a foundation based on personal beliefs and assumptions. And without a solid foundation, your entire practice might fall apart as a result.

In this chapter, we will touch on a few key points about Buddhism and why Buddhists practice to help you build your foundation of practice.

Please do not worry if you do not yet have a strong reason *why* you want to practice. Sometimes there is just something about Buddhism that you connect with or interests you. The more you learn and understand, the deeper and stronger your commitment will become.

For now, *start where you are!*

The Prison of Suffering

For a vivid analogy of *why* Buddhists practice, think of yourself being wrongly imprisoned.

- You have been in jail for many years, and are unhappy since you are not free.

- You have started to grow accustomed to the routine, and have become content at times.

- Then someone tells you that there is an open door you can walk through at any time so you can be free of this suffering and live your life as it should be.

- However, you have been so conditioned and ignorant of this truth that you've never seen this open door until they pointed it to you.

- Yet, the door still appears as a bit of a mirage.

- At a deeper level, they tell you something even more outrageous. There is no prison – you just think there is and create the conditions for it to exist in your mind!

If you were faced with these truths, wouldn't you want to walk out that door and have a peaceful and happy existence?

After all, you are in a self-imposed "mental" prison you *should not* be in. It is time to get out of jail!

However, for most of us, this fundamental truth is too much to comprehend, and we continue our lives as "normal."

For Buddhists, the Buddha's truth has become the spark that motivates them to practice "getting to that door of freedom."

While Buddhists may not always understand every single concept or teaching, they are motivated to be *free* as the Buddha taught. And with this motivation, they progress on the path building wisdom, morality, and meditative concentration.

4

The Life of a Prisoner of Saṃsāra

Let us stick with our jail and prisoner analogy. The prison we are in is called *Saṃsāra*, or the "Cycle of Rebirth." Rebirth is a key part of Buddhism because it is the reason Buddhists practice: they want to end it!

Saṃsāra is a cyclical process of birth, death, and rebirth. The process is sparked by intentional volitional actions, called *Karma*, which bind one in this process like shackles on a prisoner.

In some ways, it is like how a repeat offender keeps getting re-arrested and incarcerated repeatedly. It is an endless cycle because of their unskillful unwholesome actions.

In this prison system, your actions determine the severity of your existence. These are known as the Realms of Rebirth and are taken literally by Buddhists. Therefore, they practice creating wholesome karma and generate merits to ensure fortunate rebirths in the higher realms.

> ### *Higher Realms of Rebirth*
> *Gods or Heavenly Realm*
> *Human Realm (You are Here)*
>
> ### *Lower Realms of Rebirth*
> *Demigod Realm ("Asura")*
> *Animal Realm*
> *Hungry Ghosts Realm*
> *Hell Realm*

For example, if your actions were unwholesome in this existence, the lower realms may likely to be the next existence. Whereas if your transgressions are minor, you may find yourselves in one of the higher realms. Buddhists strive to at least remain in the Human Realm.

This is like how those who commit felony crimes may face harsh life sentences or other severe penalties. In prison, they might be placed in conditions like solitary confinement. Whereas those who have jaywalked across the street might only face a citation but no incarceration time. Even in this example, all are "prisoners" of Saṃsāra, but their conditions are different.

The belief in the West that you can become enlightened in this lifetime is mostly a Western belief. Laypersons and monastics becoming enlightened is a rare experience. Even the Buddha spent countless lifetimes practicing before he achieved enlightenment in his last existence.

For all Buddhists, the practice of the path is what is important. This means realizing that this process can span many existences and that practicing now is of the upmost importance.

Why? Because the Buddha said that the *Human Realm* is the rarest and most important of the realms of rebirth because it provides the right conditions for hearing the Dharma, practicing the Dharma, and achieving enlightenment.

The other higher realms are also beneficial but can be too far removed from the conditions found in the Human Realm that benefit enlightenment. And the lower realms make it almost impossible to hear the Dharma let alone practice it.

Therefore, Buddhists have both motivation and urgency in their practice to generate the right conditions for future rebirths. Your actions (Karma) are the only thing you have control over and are what determines rebirth.

Ultimately, ending Karma that shackles one to rebirth[3] is the goal of Buddhists. Only enlightened beings who understand the *Dependent Origination*[4] produce Karma *without* outflows and become liberated from the unsatisfactory nature of Saṃsāra.

Think of it like a reformed repeat offender who now sees the errors of their ways, no longer violates the law, and becomes completely free. That is our goal!

---

[3] Known as "Karma with Outflows". These are the "fetters" (chains or shackles) that keep on trapped in the cycle of rebirth.

[4] A Buddhist concept explaining conditionality. All phenomena do not exist independently of other things, do not have a separate independent self, and are not permanent. All phenomena arise and fall, dependent on causes and conditions.

The Four Noble Truths

All the Buddha's teachings explain the true nature of our existence and world, which is marked with something called *Dukkha*. Dukkha is sometimes referred to as "suffering" but has a myriad of meanings for something "not quite right" in our life.

Because our mind is "clouded" to this fundamental *truth* the Buddha taught, we believe suffering is our true existence and are unaware of its illusionary foundation. As a result, we create unskillful and unwholesome actions (Karma).

The Buddha said Dukkha is a *conditioned* experience which we can *end*. He taught the nature of Dukkha and how to end it with his *Four Noble Truths*. There is no reason to suffer!

The Buddha explained his teachings similar to a physician talking to a patient. But instead of explaining a medical issue, he explained the truth of Dukkha.

1. **The Truth of Suffering** ("The Symptom"): Life entails suffering (*"Dukkha / Duḥkha"*)

2. **The Cause of Suffering** ("The Diagnosis"): This suffering is caused by craving or desire (*"Trishna / Taṇhā"*)

3. **The Truth of the End of Suffering** ("The Prognosis"): There is a cure to this suffering, which helps you achieve your true natural mental state known as *Nibbāna / Nirvāṇa*

4. **The Truth of the Path That Frees of Suffering** ("The Prescription"): Follow the eightfold path to eliminate suffering in your life (*"Magga / Mārga"*)

Nicely built into the Four Truths is the **Eightfold Path** (see page 17) which "cures" you of Dukkha by leading you to your "Dukkha free" state of Nirvāṇa. This path produces *wholesome* karma because it is the actions of someone who is aligned properly with the Buddha's teachings that leads to enlightenment.

The Doorway to Freedom

By becoming awakened to the truth (*Dharma*), you can see the true nature of things – which is the conditioned, impermanent, ever changing, and interconnected nature of our world and existence.

This is the world that we previously viewed and interacted with incorrectly due to our own illusions and perceptions when unenlightened.

When you become awakened to this truth, you have eliminated delusion and ignorance and are able to cut off the resulting unwholesome Karmic actions of greed and anger which continuously forces rebirth of new existences in the cycle of rebirth (*Saṃsāra*) which is unsatisfactory (*Dukkha*).

Your true existence is free of greed, anger, and ignorance (Three Fires[5]), the Cycle of Rebirth, and Dukkha. The ending of the Three Fires is called *Nirvāṇa*.

In this enlightened state, you are unshackled (*fetters removed* – known as *Karma without outflows*) from your unskillful and unwholesome actions (*Karma*) that were leading you to constant rebirth, which is unsatisfactory.

You can then exist in the world in your true natural state free of wrong perceptions, unskillful actions, and continued forced rebirth in new existences. So, how do we get there?

All Buddhist practice is generally centered around the Buddha's Eightfold Path, which generates wholesome karma and merit leading towards ending greed, anger, and ignorance, and awakening the mental state of Nirvāṇa.

Mahāyāna Buddhism's focus is on the path of a Bodhisattva[6] and uses the *Six Perfections* (see page 18), rather than the Eightfold Path, although both are related.

---

[5] Mahāyāna also has the Five Poisons which includes Pride and Envy.

[6] An enlightened being. The Buddha was a Bodhisattva many times in prior existences, and Mahāyāna practitioners follow a similar path and goal.

What is a Daily Practice?

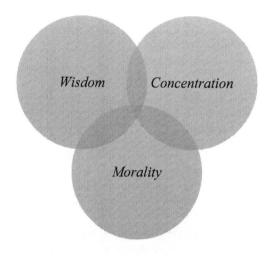

Now that we know why Buddhists practice, what does Buddhist practice consist of?

It is important to note that Buddhism is not one central religion or central set of practices. There are many different traditions[7], scriptural canons, and methods of practice. However, most Buddhist traditions have the *Threefold Training* as the foundation of their practice.

The Threefold Training is based upon the three groupings of the Buddha's Noble Eightfold Path (which can also be found in the Six Perfections of Mahāyāna).

This training helps us to create the conditions that eliminate the Three Fires of greed, anger, and ignorance which cause suffering and dissatisfaction in our lives.

When the Three Fires are "put out," we can realize the clam and peaceful mental state of Nirvāṇa that no longer creates unskillful actions and unwholesome conduct.

---

[7] Refer to page 149 to learn about the Buddhist traditions.

The *Threefold Training* consists of:

1. Understand the <u>truth about suffering</u> ("**wisdom**") through Right **Understanding** and **Thoughts**.

2. Create the <u>conditions to transcend suffering</u> ("**conduct**" or "**morality**") through Right **Speech**, **Livelihood**, and **Action**.

3. Keep on the <u>path towards awakening</u> ("**discipline**" or "**meditation**") through Right **Effort**, **Mindfulness**, and **Concentration**.

These three categories are interconnected, and when fully understood and practiced in one's life, form the right causes and conditions for awakening.

If one does not have proper cultivation of morality, meditation will not bear the right fruits. If one only studies Buddhism intellectually without also focusing on settling the mind, they cannot gain true insight.

Layperson Buddhists around the world practice this Threefold Training in many ways depending on the tradition they follow. However, the cultivation of morality and generation of merit are the most important things that many Buddhists practice in everyday life.

They will also attend ceremonies and services at a Temple where they will recite scripture (Sūtra/Sutta) or a mantra, invoke the name of a Buddha, listen to Dharma talks by a monastic, and in meditation and/or chanting.

Laypersons may attend, at least once a year, short-term retreats or even a one-day Eight Precepts retreat where they will live a modified monastic life to recharge their faith. These are some of the many different Buddhist practices that help them cultivate all three parts of the training.

You can begin learning and practicing Buddhism using the daily practice in this book, and progress to additional practices, such as retreats, when you are ready.

How Do I Practice?

What does a day in the life of a Buddhist look like?

In the morning they have a devotional practice consisting of presenting offerings, bowing and prostrations, and chanting. All of these activities generate merit (page 84).

In addition to their home practice, they are often very involved with their temple and monastics because these two things are a *refuge* for them on the Buddhist path (page 44).

At their temple, they will attend services, ceremonies, meditation, perform repentance, and other events. They form a deep and symbiotic relationship with monastics by volunteering at the temple to help with activities, cleaning, cooking, etc.

In everyday life, Buddhists practice virtue (moral conduct known as "śīla") as the foundation of the Buddhist path. This includes the Five Precepts (page 45), Eight Precepts during observance days (page 106), and generosity (page 127).

Before You Begin

Buddhist practice is an active one that encompasses all aspects of your life. You will be engaging in a wide variety of techniques such as sitting meditation, walking meditation, chanting, recitation, prostrations, handling objects, and more.

There is no way that a book could ever hope to teach you how to properly do all these things, and that includes this one.

While I have attempted to provide you an introduction to Buddhist practice here, you should only engage in these practices if you are healthy to do so and are capable. You should never push yourself to try anything that can cause you harm.

The traditional and proper approach to learning Buddhist practice is at a temple with monastics or other lay teachers. This way, you are under the guidance and observation of monastics and teachers to help ensure you are doing techniques properly. I highly encourage this approach.

While I realize that one reason you may be reading this book is because you do not have a temple nearby, there are ways to mitigate this. Some Buddhist temples have online sessions to help you practice. Another way is to visit a temple during your vacation or when you can to learn in person.

Even though you may not be able to go to temple as often as you would like, attending a retreat or class by monastics can provide the foundation for the rest of your practice at home.

Buddhist practices are not meant to resolve any medical or psychological concerns. They are religious practices for liberation from the cycle of rebirth and Dukkha.

Finally, you should be healthy to undertake a particular practice or technique. Before engaging in any activity, to include meditation and prostrations, please check with your physician to ensure that you are healthy to do so and do not have any underlying conditions. If at any time you feel unwell or unsure, consult your physician or emergency services as appropriate.

Do I Have to Be a Buddhist?

No, you do not have to be a Buddhist to practice. It is quite common for people to learn and practice Buddhism in the beginning before deciding to become an actual Buddhist. This may be where you are at right now.

This period of "investigation" or "observation" is where you are deciding if Buddhism is the path you want to follow. So, participating in the wide range of activities of Buddhism makes sense to help you with that decision. And when you are ready, you can "officially" become a Buddhist with the Triple Gem Refuge ceremony[8].

Buddhists practice because they have committed themselves to this path. And while this may seem like a blind faith, it is not.

A Buddhist's faith exists because the teachings and concepts can at times be incredibly difficult to comprehend. It can take some practitioners a lifetime to hopefully understand a concept like "emptiness" or "non-self."

They understand that they may be able to understand some concepts eventually through practice, but other things may take much longer. Not knowing everything right now is indeed "OK" and they put their faith in the Buddha.

The faith we have is like trusting a firefighter who is rescuing us from a burning building. They can "see in the dark" (or have a flashlight) and is guiding us out of the house that is filled with smoke to a door that leads to the safety of outside.

This is like the faith we have in Buddhism with the Buddha as our teacher and/or other enlightened beings, and monastics, who are guiding us with the "flashlight" of the Dharma us to the freedom of Nirvāṇa.

---

[8] Learn more: https://alanpeto.com/buddhism/triple-gem-refuge/

Building a Foundation

As you begin a Buddhist practice, the following recommendations can help you overcome some concerns.

1. Location: Find a **quiet place** in your home to practice. If you do not have someplace in your home to set up your practice, you can look for a safe place in your community or school that might be appropriate.

2. Interruptions: Don't be concerned if your practice gets **interrupted**, such as because of a phone call or visitor. Simply mark or tag your place in the daily practice steps and return to them once you are able. Depending on what step you were interrupted in, it is recommended to start that part over again (such as chanting a sūtra).

3. Frequency: Be consistent! Just like going to the gym, progress can often be subtle and not overtly apparent to you. Keep practicing!

This guide is designed to take you step-step each day through a generalized Buddhist practice to help you start.

Because there would be no way to fully explain every single Buddhist tradition's practice, you will find a balanced approach in this book that gives you a 'taste' of a few of them.

There are several options given at different points to modify the daily practice. Perhaps you want to have a more Mahāyāna specific routine, and you'll find opportunities to do that. Or, if you would like to explore a Theravāda sutta, you will have an opportunity for that.

While your goal should be to find a Buddhist tradition so you can have the guidance of monastics and follow their daily practice routine, the routine provided in these pages can help you start your Buddhist journey in a proper and respectful way.

Devotional Practice

A devotional daily practice may not be the first thing you think of for a Buddhist practice, but it the most common. In-fact, this is simply what "Buddhism" is to the half-billion Buddhists around the world.

The benefit of this practice is the ability to generate *confidence* in the Buddhist religion and path, which allows you to find *joy* on the path, *calm* because of confidence and joy, and ultimately *ease*. This provides the *foundation* for meditative concentration *leading* to insight and enlightenment.

So, what are we doing with devotional practice?

A devotional practice is designed to help with the arising of a Buddha or Bodhisattva in our minds through various practices.

This is important because when we have a teacher we respect around us, we are less likely to engage in unskillful and unwholesome actions.

Just imagine if the Buddha was physically in front of you and was your teacher in this world. Would you want to deviate from the path he set forth? Would you pay attention as he spoke? Would you try to journey to where he is teaching and listen to him?

When we have faith, trust, reverence, and devotion to something wholesome that we respect and feel strongly about, like a Buddha, then that is something we want to bring with us into our practice.

Buddhists are devotional to the *Triple Gem* which consists of the Buddha as the teacher, the Dharma as his liberating path and teachings, and the Sangha as the monastic community.

What makes one a Buddhist is traditionally taking "refuge" in this Triple Gem because it is the path we want to follow.

We may not fully understand all the Buddhist terminology, concepts, teachings, and practices, but we do not have to when we are first starting out. And that's where devotional Buddhism helps us.

A devotional practice is easy to begin and remain consistent on. This is key because Buddhism is not something you do "when I feel like it" but is a daily exercise.

After setting up a simple altar, you can engage in a practice that consists of (but not limited to):

- **Bowing** before a Buddha or Bodhisattva(s).

- **Providing offerings** (water, candle/light, etc.).

- **Chant** (in Mahāyāna, a common practice is to chant the Heart Sūtra) and / or recite the name of a Buddha (such as Gautama or Amitābha) or a Bodhisattva.

While this seems overly simplistic, it accomplishes several things:

1. Helps you to align your mind with the Buddha's teachings ("Dharma" or "Buddhadharma") which is the path towards liberation or freedom from suffering.

2. Breaks down the ego and attachment to the idea of self through practicing charity, kindness, and compassion.

3. Helps to slowly "polish" the figurative mirror that helps you see and realize your true inner nature (which is Nirvāṇa).

4. Transforms your morality and conduct to be aligned with what the Buddha taught, and enlightened beings such as Buddhas, Bodhisattvas, and Arhats.

Many laypersons use their devotional practice to show compassion and loving-kindness towards loved ones, especially those who have passed away by dedicating merits generated because of the practice.

The Eightfold Path

Following the Buddha's Noble Eightfold Path allows us to end Dukkha caused by the unskillful and unwholesome actions resulting from our greed, anger, and ignorance.

1. **Right View:** The ability to have right concepts and right ideas that lead away from delusion and wrong views.

2. **Right Thought:** Keeping thoughts in accord with the Buddha's Dharma. This is the "speech of your mind", therefore you want to ensure your thoughts align with Right View.

3. **Right Speech:** Ensuring your "verbal" Karma consists of words of truth, compassion, praise, and altruism.

4. **Right Action:** Ensuring your "bodily" Karma consists of not killing, not stealing, and not engaging in sexual misconduct.

5. **Right Livelihood:** Having the right occupation in life that does not harm others and ourselves.

6. **Right Effort:** Dilligence in preventing unwholesome states that have yet to arisen, ending unwholesome states that have arisen, and strengthening wholesome states.

7. **Right Mindfulness:** True contemplation where the mind is pure, aware, and does not give rise to unwholesome thoughts.

8. **Right Concentraiton:** Using samādhi (meditative concentration) to focus the mind and settle the distracted body in order to develop insight *(Pāli: vipassanā / Sanskrit: vipaśyanā)* so one can become enlightened to the truth.

The Six Perfections

Although Mahāyāna Buddhism has the Eightfold Path as a foundational teaching, it places emphasis on cultivating the Six Perfections (Pāramitās) as the primary practice.

These Six Perfections are the path of a *Bodhisattva* who is striving to become a Buddha because these perfections are the qualities of an enlightened being

While they may appear different than the Eightfold Path, they correlate to it. The Six Perfections can be understood in one way as the cumulation of what the Eightfold Path is helping us achieve.

The Six Perfections are:

1. *The perfection of **Giving***

2. *The perfection of **Morality***

3. *The perfection of **Patience***

4. *The perfection of **Diligence***

5. *The perfection of **Meditative Concentration***

6. *The perfection of **Prajñā-Wisdom***

For Mahāyānists, the development of these perfections, along with the Bodhisattva Vow and cultivation of Bodhicitta (enlightened mind), constitutes the disciplined "path" of a Bodhisattva that is working their way towards Buddhahood.

While each of these perfections appear straightforward, they must always be combined with the sixth perfection: Prajñā.

Prajñā is direct insight of wisdom. It ensures you perform the other five perfections in the correct way, and not as one who is captivated by wrong views.

A simple way to understand these perfections is to envision the Buddha and how he interacted with others, the world, and his practice. Prajñā *is* the enlightened state of a Buddha.

How Do I Stay Motivated?

Do nothing that is unwholesome.
Do all that is wholesome.
Purify the mind.
This is the teaching of all Buddhas.

A consequence of any type of practice, study, or exercise can be "burnout" or "apathy."

To stay motivated, the best practice of all is to be engaged with a Buddhist temple and community to support and motivate you.

The ability to practice with other *Dharma friends* (see page 145) is invaluable and a very traditional approach. The support and structure you will receive will make all the difference. Like having a partner that you work out with at a gym, the same can be found in Buddhist practice.

However, if you do not have a temple nearby, and are practicing Buddhism only at home and online, the tendency to "take a break" or "find something else to do" will be strong.

Some strategies to keep motivated will depend on your own personal temperament and preferences.

Here are a few you can use:

1. Practice devotional Buddhism (see page 15).

2. Use an app or alarm on your smartphone to remind you to practice at set times and to track it so you can be motivated by keeping a consistent practice streak.

3. Many temples have livestream events. You can usually 'subscribe' to be notified when livestream events will take place.

4. Join online groups where other practitioners form a layperson community to share advice, guidance, and support. A temple you join may have social groups for their lay practitioners on social media platforms.

5. Do not overcommit or try to do too much with your practice. Consistency is the key; not how much you try to do all at once. Just like going to the gym, trying to lift weights that are too heavy for you will only cause you to be injured and lose interest in going to the gym. The same adage holds true for Buddhism.

My advice to you on how to keep motivated it is to understand *why* we practice.

As I mentioned previously, we are like prisoners in this unsatisfactory existence (refer to page 4). Why would you want to remain a prisoner?

Or why would you want to be burned by fire (an analogy for the Three Fires of greed, anger, and ignorance)?

The vast majority of Buddhists practice Buddhism to create the right conditions for future rebirths by generating merit with their practice. This very real fear of facing rebirth in the lower realms of rebirth is an extraordinarily strong motivator.

Even if you are not fully accepting of the realms of rebirth now, you can apply it to your everyday life. The realms of rebirth can also correlate to your mental state and actions.

Do you want to always be clinging and craving like a hungry ghost? Do you want to always be suffering painfully like in a hell realm due to your actions?

Whatever your personal motivation is for practicing Buddhism, keeping it forefront in your practice. Even if this means writing it on a note card and keeping it on your altar to remind you!

Daily Practice Motivational Poster

The Buddha said that the Human realm of rebirth (where you are right now) is the most precious, rare, and important one to be reborn into. This is because it is an existence where we have not only freewill but experience the right conditions and motivations to practice Buddhism.

Because you experience both pleasure and suffering in this realm, you are likely to be spurred into action with practicing Buddhism. The other realms are often to the extremes and do not provide this crucial balance we find here. Think of it like baking a soufflé. You need the right ingredients, patience, conditions, and skills to ensure it bakes just right.

The Buddha also said this human existence is rare. If you do not practice here now, it can be a *very* long time before you have a chance again. And then, it may be an existence where Buddhist teachings have been lost and will not be rediscovered for a while.

To aid us with our daily practice I have created a simple poster you can refer to with one of the most famous teachings of the Buddha found in both branches of Buddhism.

At the beginning of this chapter, you were introduced to a quote attributed to the Buddha in both the *Dhammapada* (verse 183) and the *Verse of the Seven Ancient Buddhas*[9]. It succinctly explains what one should do in their Buddhist practice.

While this verse seems simplistic, the actual meaning of it, and practice to achieve it, is rigorous and requires constant effort.

The first part of the verse is regarding our morality, conduct, and actions (karma). This is what we must change.

---

[9] The verse here is from the Seven Ancient Buddhas; however, it is very similar to Dhammapada verse 183. There are many translations which you can find online or in books which all have the same underlying meaning. You can find a printable version of this poster as part of the PDF book download at https://alanpeto.com/books

We want to engage on the path towards enlightenment in ways that are wholesome, not unwholesome. Otherwise, we are simply creating the same conditions that are keeping us trapped in an unsatisfactory existence.

How do we do this? Purify the mind, the Buddha says. When we can purify the mind of greed, anger, and ignorance (Three Fires / Three Poisons), we no longer create unwholesome actions.

Whenever I read this verse, I am motivated that these enlightened teachers (Buddhas) can easily distill what we need to do and provides us the path to achieve it!

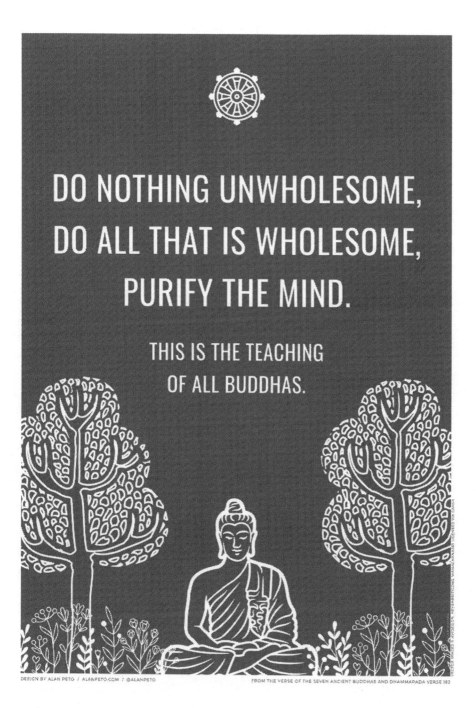

My Motivation

      Use this space to record your motivation for practicing Buddhism. This is a beneficial practice to help you know where you are starting from, and where you find yourself at set points.

      If your motivation ever changes, you can come back here to reflect upon your journey so you can reinvigorate it.

Now

Why I want to practice Buddhism:

_____

_____

_____

_____

How do you feel?

❑ Motivated ❑ Struggling ❑ Interested ❑ Unsure

Triple Gem Refuge

At the time of your Triple Gem Refuge, reflect on why you decided to officially become a Buddhist:

_____

_____

_____

_____

How do you feel?

❑ Motivated ❑ Struggling ❑ Interested ❑ Unsure

24

At Six Months

Why I continue to practice Buddhism:

_____

_____

_____

_____

How do you feel?

❑ Motivated ❑ Struggling ❑ Interested ❑ Unsure

At One Year

My motivation to continue practicing Buddhism:

_____

_____

_____

_____

How do you feel?

❑ Motivated ❑ Struggling ❑ Interested ❑ Unsure

Notes & Insights

_____

_____

_____

_____

_____

Daily Practice Quick Start

These steps will be the basis of the daily practice explained in this book. Each step will be explained more fully, however this quick start can be used to help you remember and follow the steps. Start with the steps you feel comfortable with and explore other steps of the practice if/when you are ready.

If you are short on time, a quick session can consist of 1) providing an offering(s), 2) paying homage to the Buddha by bowing three times, and/or 3) reciting the Buddha's name (bow and/or prostrate each time).

Please be sure to read the notice on page 12 before starting.

Step 1: Bow/Prostrate & Provide Offering(s)

- Join your palms and bow before a statue or illustration of a Buddha or a Bodhisattva. You can then provide an offering(s) in front of the statue:

    o   Flower
    o   Water
    o   Fruit
    o   Burn Incense
    o   Light a Candle

Step 2: Take Refuge in the Triple Gem

- *"I take refuge in the Buddha,*
- *"I take refuge in the Dharma,*
- *"I take refuge in the Sangha"*

Step 3: Recite the Five Precepts

- *"I will refrain from taking life,*
- *"I will refrain from stealing or taking what is not freely given,*
- *"I will refrain from sexual misconduct,*
- *"I will refrain from false speech, and*
- *"I will refrain from consuming intoxicants and stimulants."*

Step 4: Recite the Five Remembrances

- *"I am subject to aging. There is no way to avoid aging.*
- *"I am subject to ill health. There is no way to avoid illness.*
- *"I am going to die. There is no way to avoid death.*
- *"Everyone and everything that I love will change, and I will be separated from them.*
- *"My only true possessions are my actions, and I cannot escape their consequences."*

Step 5: Recite, Chant, or Read Scripture (Sūtra)

- There are several examples to choose from in the book.

- Most Mahāyāna Buddhists recite the Heart Sūtra, although there are other popular ones depending on tradition. Note that if you use a short Sūtra, such as the Heart Sūtra, your daily practice may be around five minutes in length.

Step 6: Meditate or Chant

- Note that if you are doing a quick five-minute daily practice, exclude this portion if you have already chanted a short Sūtra, such as the Heart Sūtra.
- For meditation, begin by straightening your spine & relax the muscles in your body.
- There are various meditative practices, however counting the breath is a popular practice for beginners. Perform one count for the inhalation and another count for the exhalation. Count to ten and start over. If you forget your count, simply start over. As you quiet the mind, keep maintaining awareness of the breath.
- During your meditation, observe any thoughts arising in your mind and let them go.
- You can also quickly recite the name of a Buddha, such as Amitābha Buddha, three times with your full attention. This constitutes a form of contemplative meditation or recitation (see page 82).

Step 7: Dedicate Merits of Practice

"For all sentient beings, I dedicate the meritorious actions of this practice so they may be guided and liberated from delusion and suffering with the light of the Buddha's Dharma."

Daily Practice Tracking

     Remaining consistent is important for Buddhist practice. You can use this page to track yourself for the first month.

     Checkmark each day you have completed using the steps in this chapter. Use a pencil if you would like to reuse this calendar.

     You can also use the calendar to track the guided practice found later in this book (refer to page 91), and how you felt about it. For example, the practice for "Day 1" would be "1" and you can use a rating scale of 1 through 5 (with 5 being the best) on how your practice was. Example: 1-5.

1	2	3	4	5	6	7
8	9	10	11	12	13	14
15	16	17	18	19	20	21
22	23	24	25	26	27	28
29	30	31				

Step 1: Offerings and Prostrations

A traditional part of practice is to bow and prostrate before a Buddha or Bodhisattva and give offerings.

Bowing, prostrations, and offerings are done as a sign of generosity, devotion, humility, and respect, *not* as a form of worship.

This practice is usually done at the beginning of a practice but may also be done during reciting the Triple Gem, and when entering the main shrine at a temple.

Because our ego is so strong, we may scoff at doing such a practice. However, this helps us with breaking the attachment and love of the idea of "self" and transforming the mind to be compassionate and skillful.

When you bow before a Buddha, you are symbolically bowing to the Buddha that is inside you!

Buddha statues are not only symbolic of a Buddha, who is a teacher, but also a reflection of what already exists within you that you are working to reveal. All sentient beings inherently have "Buddha nature" meaning we all have the innate capability to become enlightened.

The examples provided here are illustrating a general way to bow, prostrate, and provide offerings, until you decide upon a tradition which will give you their preferred method.

If you have already decided on a tradition to follow, how you bow, prostrate, and provide offers should be what you follow.

Opening Prayers

We will discuss prayers performed at the end of our practice later when we discuss dedicating merits.

However, opening prayers are common in Buddhist traditions to begin your daily practice with the correct mindset.

If you wish to incorporate this practice, you can explore what's available from Buddhist temples and monastics online to determine what you'd like to use. You may also consider the Triple Gem and Five Precepts featured in this book as a form of prayer.

To give another example, Mahāyāna Buddhists who have taken the Bodhisattva precepts may have an opening prayer which is reciting the four great Bodhisattva Vows:

Sentient beings are numberless, I vow to save them
Desires are inexhaustible, I vow to end them
Dharma gates are boundless, I vow to enter them
The Buddha's way is unsurpassable, I vow to become it.

Hands

Your hands will be in the "praying" form (two hands together) while being slightly cupped and thumbs parallel with your other fingers (don't let them stick out like a "thumbs up").

Depending on tradition, your thumbs may be tucked inside your cupped hands to be visually symbolic of a lotus flower bud. Lotus flowers are used extensively in Buddhism because they are reflective of the different stages of the Buddhist path, and enlightenment.

Bowing

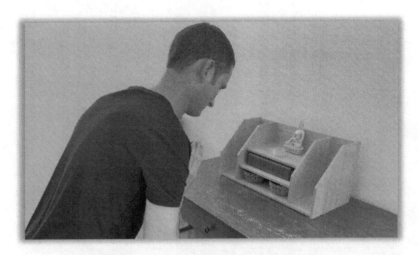

Buddhists may bow before a Buddha three times for the Triple Gem (the Buddha, the Dharma, and the Sangha).

If you do not have a statue or picture of the Buddha, you can use the one provided on the next page.

Keep your hands generally around chest level, and bend at your waist as you bow. Depending on tradition, you may also bring your hands up to your forehead and back to your chest.

After you bow, you may want to perform prostrations which are explained in this chapter.

Depending on the tradition, ceremony, or event, you may be doing a few, or up to 108 prostrations as part of the practice.

Do not worry about rushing into such large repetitions initially. Start with a number of bowing and/or prostrations that are comfortable for you and work your way up.

Prostrations

The purpose of prostrations is to show devotion and respect to a Buddha or Bodhisattva for their teachings and help, and to practice humility.

This can be a new and unbalancing technique, so ensure you are healthy and safe to do this and learn this at a temple if possible. The steps shown here is just one method.

For a quick practice, perform three prostrations, then one more standing bow at the end to conclude. You may decide to eventually work your way up to 108 prostrations.

1. Begin standing upright. Your hands will be in the praying position close to your chest.

2. Transition from your standing "praying" hand position to going to your knees. Place your right hand on the mat while keeping your left hand the praying position close to your chest. Note that if you are left-handed, you can reverse this process if that is easier for you.

3. Next, move your left hand so it aligned with your head.

4. Move your right hand so it is parallel with your left.

5. Place your forehead on the mat so your hands are close and slightly in front of your head. Rest your torso so your body is close to or touching your thighs. Your back will be rounded, not straight. You will be in a position where your buttocks will be resting on your legs and the toes of your feet will be close (almost touching each other). Your forearms will be touching the ground/mat.

6. Begin to slowly turn your palms up. Your hands are held like a fist, but looser.

7. Turn your palms up. Fingers slightly curled or straight.

8. To complete the prostration, you will need to return to the standing position by reversing these steps.

    a. Turn your hands back so your palms are on the mat.
    b. Move your right hand back to steady your body.
    c. Slowly and carefully begin to stand.
    d. Your left hand will be in the praying position again.
    e. Continue the process of standing.
    f. Right hand meets the left in the praying position.
    g. Bow.

Offerings

Part of a Buddhist practice may include presenting offerings to a Buddha, a Bodhisattva, and monastics.

The types of offerings range from material offerings, such as lighting incense, giving food and water, flowers, or lighting a candle, to non-material offerings ("practice offerings") consisting of moral conduct, meditation, and wisdom.

Why do we give offerings? It is a practice to help us develop and show compassion and loving-kindness and purify ourselves of ignorance and delusion.

As you do this, with correct intent, you are planting seeds within yourself that allow compassion and loving-kindness to "bloom" beyond just where you practice.

Buddhist practice, which includes offerings, are part of *merit generation / cultivation* which encompass a large part of what laypersons do. Merit helps ensure a favorable rebirth that is conducive to the path towards enlightenment, and conditions in this current existence.

For a daily practice, an offering can be provided in a small bowl to keep your altar space tidy. It is a customary practice to incorporate bowing as you provide offerings.

Water Offering

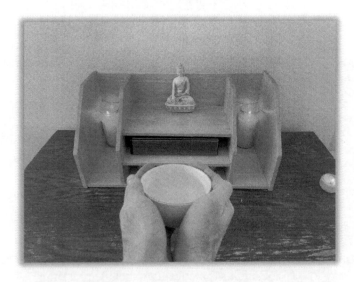

- Depending on the shape of the container, cup it with your hands like you are holding a bowl.

- Present to the Buddha, and then place carefully in front of the Buddha and/or altar.

- The offering of water is symbolic of generosity, charity, and kindness.

- The water presented may be "perfumed" with a scent or remain unscented.

Light Offering

- Depending on the shape and type of light offering, you can hold the base with your fingers. For larger candles or containers, keep it steady and safe.

- One practice you can use is to lift the candle up towards and in front of your forehead *(ensuring the candle and flame are not close to your head, hair, etc., for safety)* as you present it to the Buddha. Then bring it back in front of you around chest level. Place in front of the Buddha and/or altar.

- This act is symbolic of the desire for the "light" of wisdom as it relates to enlightenment.

What about incense? Even though we initially light an incense stick with a flame, the flame is put out and only smoke remains. Therefore, it is considered a different type of offering.

With incense, it's generally symbolic of purifying the space you are practicing in. There are many ways of offering incense. If you are offering incense at a temple, please ask them first. There may be etiquette on how to offer, and a limit on how many incense sticks you can use.

The Ten Offerings

There are many types of offerings that can be presented to a Buddha or Bodhisattva.

While there can be some variation of types of offerings between the different traditions, the following list can provide some examples of what may be presented:

1. **Incense**

2. **Flowers**

3. **Lamps (Light)**

4. **Ointments**

5. **Fruit**

6. **Tea**

7. **Food**

8. **Treasures**

9. **Beads**

10. **Clothing**

Each offering type is typically symbolic to the conditions and path in Buddhism. For example, lamp or light offerings are symbolic of wisdom and enlightenment.

They also have a dual purpose to help with the daily running of the temple, needs of monastics, etc.

You will notice at many temples there are Buddhist laypersons providing these offerings. At larger temples, there may be the opportunity to provide a donation to use offerings already prepared for you to give.

If you are unsure of how to give an offering at a temple, just ask! The monastic or volunteer will show you the correct way to provide the offering.

Step 2: The Three Refuges

I take refuge in the Buddha

I take refuge in the Dharma

I take refuge in the Sangha

What is the Triple Gem?

One officially becomes a Buddhist by taking the Triple Gem Refuge in the Buddha, his teachings (Dharma), and the monastic community (Sangha). In a daily practice, one may recite the Three Refuges to gain strength and support and to reaffirm their commitment to the Buddhist path.

Why is it Part of a Daily Practice?

The reason we recite the Three Refuges (Triple Gem) in our daily practice is to center ourselves and practice on these three precious things that help lead us to enlightenment.

The Triple Gem are indeed precious "gems" that are beyond any mundane monetary value. This is because the three of them are wholesome and are interconnected to help us achieve enlightenment and Nirvāṇa.

When we recite the Triple Gem, we are reminding ourselves of their importance, and our faith and commitment.

While this may appear unnecessary to some, the practice helps us with taming our ego (where we might think we "know it all" and can "do it by ourselves") and turning our vision to the three things that have a proven impact to laypersons and monastics on the path.

Step 3: The Five Precepts

I will refrain from Killing, Harming, or Violating Others

I will refrain from Stealing or Taking What is Not Mine

I will refrain from Sexual Misconduct

I will refrain from Lying, Gossip, or Harsh Speech

I will refrain from Intoxicants or Stimulants

What Is the Meaning of the Five Precepts?

The *Five Precepts* provide us a distillation of the *Vinaya*, which are the rules for monastics. However, the Five Precepts applies to *all* Buddhists.

When you decide to take the precepts, you are saying these are the things you aspire towards. Because precepts help you progress on the path towards enlightenment through the cultivation of right conduct, they are accepted as a part of a Buddhist's life.

A Buddhist *willingly* takes on these precepts either at the time of their Triple Gem ceremony, or when their faith and understanding develops.

When one abides by the precepts, they are performing good deeds and living their life aligned with morality and conduct as the Buddha taught.

Precepts provide us the path to help us abide with the morality and conduct portion of the Eightfold Path.

Without precepts, the wisdom and concentration portions of the Eightfold Path would not have a solid foundation for us to follow the Buddha's teachings.

Rules or Direction?

"Don't tell me what to do!" you might be thinking. Rest assured; the Buddha is <u>not</u> telling you what to do.

These are precepts for those who want to take them – meaning *Buddhists*. They are a welcomed part of the path for one who wants to earnestly make progress.

You willingly decide to take the precepts to benefit yourself on the path. They are all there for a purpose, which is to help you correctly follow the Threefold Training.

Following the precepts is *freedom*. Not only the freedom the Buddhist path leads us to, but the freedom from the unwholesome and unsatisfactory conditions the absence of following the precepts cause.

Now, nobody is perfect, so when you recite these, you are saying you have the aspiration and intention to follow them and will to the best of your ability. Remember, intentions matter!

Sometimes we are in places or situations which make these exceedingly difficult to follow. Even the Buddha's followers had similar situations. The key point is they made the efforts to eventually get to this level, or as close to it as possible. That is something we can all strive for.

The repercussions for breaking the precepts result in unwholesome karmic imprints which are unwanted in the Buddhist religion because they hinder someone trying to reach enlightenment.

The Five Precepts often mirror societal law which is another reason Buddhists abide by them. In our secular world, breaking laws can result in severe repercussions such as criminal and civil charges.

What If You Break a Precept?

Violating any of these precepts means we have deviated from the Buddhist path (and the Threefold Training) to freedom. When that happens, we need to reflect on what we did, and how it conflicts with the Buddha's teachings.

If you do accidentally violate one of these precepts, there is no supernatural being that will punish you. Karmic actions are your own, wholesome or unwholesome, and precepts are there to help guide you towards the wholesome side of things.

There are two types of violations of the precepts. *Parajika* is for *major or grave* offenses where the violation is not easily committed (such as the taking of a life). *Duskrta* is for *minor* offenses or misdeeds such as accidentally stepping on a bug.

With Duskrta you can sincerely repent to address the misdeed. This can include repenting before the Buddha, vow taking (such as reaffirming to uphold that precept in the future), merit generation, etc.

Repentance is designed to help you identify the unethical behavior (to develop Right View) so you can prevent future violations, and sincerely repent for what occurred.

This repentance is done to address the Buddhist focus of the precepts where we are cultivating right conduct and morality.

While precepts *may* mirror societal law in various ways, Buddhist repentance is not meant to legally address any violations of the law. Precepts and repentance are for Buddhists to address a religious purpose to create the right conditions for enlightenment.

Some transgressions of the precepts, such as killing a living being intentionally (which would be a major offense), cannot have those karmic seeds or results resolved through repentance.

Bodhisattva Precepts

The Five Precepts are like the entry-level rules for a Buddhist. Like being in school, as one advances in grade levels, more is required to eventually reach "graduation". The same holds true when one takes on additional precepts.

In addition to the Five Precepts, Mahāyāna Buddhists often vow to uphold the *Bodhisattva Precepts* (refer to page 112). If you have taken the Bodhisattva Precepts as a layperson, you should incorporate them into your practice during this step.

To aid in this practice, Mahāyānists may use the *"Three Pure Precepts"* during their practice as a distillation of the path of a Bodhisattva.

While it is similar to the verse of the Buddhas (see page 21), the last line is replaced to highlight the aspiration of all Bodhisattvas which is to save all sentient beings.

> *To do no evil;*
> *To do good;*
> *To save all beings.*

The Three Pure Precepts seem very simple and straightforward, but they are remarkably challenging for even experienced Buddhists to achieve. This is yet another reason we practice!

Feel free to use these Three Pure Precepts if they are easier for you to remember. Their straightforward message can even be used when you are interacting with others in everyday life (refer to page 127).

Eight Precepts

Buddhist monastics often have hundreds of precepts to follow to aid them on the path to enlightenment.

Buddhist laypersons may undertake the *Eight Precepts* on special observance days to reinforce their practice and live with just two additional precepts that a monastic follows (refer to page 108).

While there is a longstanding tradition on when to observe these additional precepts (and practices), you can practice on day(s) of your choosing, or during special retreats hosted by your temple (refer to page 114).

This is not something you need to do every day (although some do); however, it is a time-honored layperson practice that allows us to practice in some of the discipline and practices monastics undertake.

Step 4: The Five Remembrances

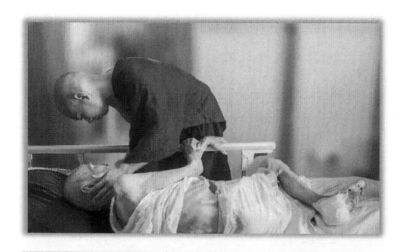

I am of the nature to grow old.
There is no way to escape growing old.

I am of the nature to have ill-health.
There is no way to escape having ill-health.

I am of the nature to die.
There is now way to escape death.

All that is dear to me and everyone I love are of the
nature to change. *There is no way to escape being*
separated from them.

I inherit the results of my actions in body, speech,
and mind. *My actions are the ground on which I stand.*

What Are the Remembrances?

The Five Remembrances (or Five Reflections) are a beautiful practice of millions of Buddhists. But they may not seem that way at first!

These can seem dreary, scary, and un-nerving. This is because they are showing us our fears, but also give us a way to face those fears head on.

The Five Remembrances are our first step onto the Eightfold Path, so it is a reason why we have it as a daily practice. When we recite the Five Remembrances, we are confronting our fears so we can transform them, and in-turn, can follow the Eightfold Path to enlightenment.

The Significance of the Remembrances

Siddhārtha Gautama's "Four Sights" (which spurred him to take the path that eventually led him to becoming the Buddha) are featured in the Five Remembrances as the **first three** items.

That is important because it was these "sights" that fundamentally shocked Siddhārtha to his core and prompted him to seek the path towards enlightenment. Now that sounds like a great reason why we recite them every day!

The **Fourth** Remembrance is directly tied to the Buddhist teaching on Impermanence. Buddhists focus their entire practice not just on removing the illusion of self, but also with deeply understanding impermanence.

The **Fifth** Remembrance is empowering. It tells us that we, and not anything or anyone else, have full control over our actions. While we cannot escape the consequences of our actions, we can ensure they are wholesome, and not unwholesome.

Step 5: Chant or Read a Sūtra

Opening Verse Before Reading Sūtras

The unsurpassed, profound, and wondrous Dharma is difficult and rare to encounter even in hundreds of thousands of millions of kalpas[10]. Since we are now able to see, hear, receive, and retain it, may I realize and comprehend the true meaning of the Buddha's truth.

---

[10] *Kalpa is an exceptionally long period of time (millions or billions of years).*

Sūtras Available Within This Book

Included in this book are six different scriptures you can use for your daily practice. Depending on your tradition, you may only use one of these, or other ones.

You can also rotate these so you can have a new Sūtra to read each day.

To aid the Westerner who is new to Buddhism, these Sūtras have been modified to make them easier to read and follow. You can find other traditional translations online.

1. **The Heart Sūtra** - Page 62

2. **The Discourse on the Blessings** - Page 64

3. **The Loving Kindness Sermon** - Page 66

4. **The Diamond Sūtra (4 Line Verse)** - Page 67

5. **The Fire Sermon** - Page 67

6. **The Eight Realizations of Great Beings** – Page 69

Ideally, you should be chanting or reciting in one of the traditional (Pāli or Sanskrit) or country-specific languages. When you chant in one of these languages, it flows more quickly, smoothly, and rhythmically than in English.

While it may sound counterproductive, it is not important to understand what is being chanted when you perform it with another language. This is because the practice itself is having a transformative effect on you, and even others who may be hearing it.

In several traditions and countries, laypersons chant in languages they do not understand, such as Pali or Sanskrit, so you will not be alone in performing it this way.

If you progress to chanting in another language, be sure to read the scripture beforehand in your language, such as English. This will allow you to "understand" the translation, and thus the meaning of what you are chanting.

Why Chant?

The historical context of chanting dates to ancient times when monastics would memorize and recite the sermons.

The written scriptures we have now were not even considered until hundreds of years after the Buddha's death. But why is there chanting now that we have written sermons?

Reading the sūtras just to gain information from them will only get you so far. The profound meaning of the teachings found in them can sometimes take a lifetime to truly understand.

When we chant the sūtras, we are going beyond conventional understanding of what is being read. Instead, it is meant to provide a unique Buddhist religious experience that allows us to gain fundamental insight to the teaching itself.

This insight may take years of repeated chanting!

Chanting can sound different depending on the tradition you are in, what is being chanted, and where.

Overall, chanting out loud is the preferred method because you are allowing those words in the sūtra to be planted like seeds in your subconscious mind.

The more you chant with consistent frequency, the more opportunities you allow your mind to absorb and discover the fundamental meaning of the sūtra and develop wisdom that leads to awakening.

Buddhists may focus on one, or several sūtras as the focus of their practice for this very purpose. While I will provide you a few in this book, you can just focus on one for your daily practice.

How Do You Chant?

Chanting is one of the most popular forms of practice for Buddhist laypersons.

Sitting meditation by laypersons is mostly a modern practice that was never routinely practiced. However, laypersons now have the time to meditate as well, which can be a beneficial part of your practice.

When you chat, your focus should not be on trying to "understand" it, which is a natural human tendency. The purpose is to create a consistent practice where religious insight can occur through this repetitive practice.

When chanting, your rhythm, tone, and tempo is typically what may appear to be "robotic" in nature.

When attending services at a temple, you will notice the liturgy for chanting has special symbols and breaks in it to indicate when each word (or part of a word) is chanted, and a particular chanting rhythm.

For example, let us look at the Heart Sūtra:

> *Sariputra, form is not different from emptiness, emptiness is not different from form*

While how you chant can vary from tradition, here is a general example of how you would break it up:

> *Sar-i-pu-tra, form is not diff-er-ent from em-pti-ness, em-pti-ness is not diff-er-ent from form*

As you chant, there is a connection between all of these 'breaks' so it flows together but is still rhythmic, such as (phonetically) "SarEEpooTRA."

In some traditions, you will even see chanting takes on a melodic flair at times depending on that part in a service. This may contrast compared to the example given here which is just a general way to chant.

For a home practice, chanting or recitation is usually done fast, but mindfully. You can, of course, chant or recite slowly or even silently.

Ensure you uphold the reverence of the sūtras by only chanting or reciting in a respectful place such as where your home altar is located (page 131). For example, you wouldn't want to take the sūtra and chant in a bathroom.

You will typically be in a sitting meditation position, kneeling, or standing when holding the sūtras.

It is recommended that you hear and observe how to chant at the temple, or in lieu of going to a temple, with a video or audio via the internet. Several Buddhist temples often have their services online which can help you understand the tempo and structure, or you can view my five-minute daily practice video[11].

Chanting in English (or your native language) typically is not ideal for Buddhist sūtras, but it can be done. When you are ready, and have found a tradition you are following, transition to chanting in the language they use.

As an important reminder, if you have difficulty chanting due to a health issue, speak with your physician or professional. Chanting should never be done if it impairs your health or breathing.

---

[11] Refer to https://alanpeto.com to view Alan's videos.

What Sūtras to Chant?

Buddhist scriptures (Sūtra/Sutta) are vast and can easily take a lifetime to not only read, but also understand.

The different Buddhist traditions have a variety of ways to incorporate Sūtras into our practice. While reading Sūtras, or hearing a Dharma talk are one way, chanting is more common.

For some traditions, either one or a few Sūtras are focused on by laypersons not only due to brevity, but as a form of practice itself. Some Sūtras, especially in Mahāyāna, may be considered all-encompassing of the goal and teachings of a particular tradition that they can be focused on almost entirely.

- For **Mahāyāna Buddhists**, the **Heart Sūtra** is perhaps the most recited Sūtra not just due to its short length, but profound meaning.

- The **Lotus Sūtra**, which is also the only Sūtra for Nichiren Buddhists, is also respected elsewhere in Mahāyāna.

- Some of the overall popular Sūtras in Mahāyāna are the **Heart**, **Diamond**, and **Lotus** Sūtras.

- Some Sūtras that are that influential with Chán/Zen traditions include the **Decent into Lanka** (Lankavatara), **Lotus**, **Diamond**, and **Flower Garland** (Avatamsaka) Sūtras.

- Pure Land Buddhism typically feature the three sūtras of **Amitābha** (Shorter and Longer) and **Meditation**.

For **Theravāda Buddhists**, these three Suttas may be considered essential reading and may be chanted. They cover fundamental teachings of the Buddha which are the core of Buddhist practice:

- **"Setting the Wheel of Dhamma in Motion"** (Dhammacakkappavattana Sutta)

- **"The Discourse of the Not-Self Characteristic"** (Anatta-lakkhana Sutta)

- **"The Fire Sermon"** (Ādittapariyāya Sutta)

Additional Suttas that may not necessarily be chanted, but will help the new Buddhist with core teachings and concepts regardless of Buddhist tradition:

- **Sigalovada Sutta:** The Buddha provides instructions for laypersons.

- **Anapānasati Sutta:** Teaching on breath meditation.

- **Maha-Satipatthana Sutta:** Teaching on mindfulness.

- **Sabbasava Sutta:** Overcoming external influences that pollute the mind.

- **Ambalatthika-rahulovada Sutta:** Teaching on Virtue.

- **Samadhanga Sutta:** Teaching on Concentration.

- **Dhatu-vibhanga Sutta:** Teaching on Wisdom.

- **Karaniya Metta Sutta:** The practice of loving-kindness.

How to Hold Sūtras

There are different ways to handle sūtras. Regardless of if you use the version shot here or not, be respectful and handle sūtras as something valuable – because Buddhists treat it as such.

1. With clean hands, hold the sūtra/liturgy/book with your thumbs and pointer fingers on top. Use your middle fingers to provide the foundation in the back.

2. You may now angle your hands and sūtra so it is parallel with the ground as you raise it to your head where your eyes are.

3. When chanting (book open or holding paper) you can use two fingers to hold it securely (with rest of your fingers providing support beneath).

4. When finished, place the book or paper respectfully in an appropriate place so it will not be damaged.

5. For another variation of holding sūtras, you can cusp the sūtras/book like you are praying. Keep your thumbs on top to hold the paper, and the rest of your fingers beneath it in the praying position

Selected Sūtras for Chanting

In the following pages you will find six Sūtras you can use as part of your daily practice. You may choose only one, or all of the following, to chant, recite, read, or contemplate.

Feel free to include your own Sūtra(s) in lieu of those provided in this guide.

Sūtras/Suttas found in this guide may have various degrees of modifications made by me to make them shorter for this daily practice, and more understandable to those new to Buddhism. However, they may be different than what is found in a scriptural canon. Perform an internet search (or your temple) to find more traditional translations if desired.

- The **Heart Sūtra** is a popular Sūtra by most traditions in East-Asian Buddhism (China, Taiwan, Vietnam, Japan, Korea) and Central-Asian Buddhism (Tibet, Bhutan, etc.). This is also a popular Sūtra to chant.

- The **Diamond Sūtra**, which is also popular in Mahāyāna, has a short "four-line verse" which is chanted and is included here. The full Diamond Sūtra may be chanted as well; however, it is much longer and may be a better choice to be chanted during observance days.

- The **other sermons** are found in both the Pali Canon (Theravāda) and Chinese Canon (East-Asian/Mahāyāna) and I have included a few here that you may enjoy as part of your daily practice.

You are not limited to just these sūtras! Feel free to explore the many scriptures available and select the ones you wish to chant.

When you decide upon a tradition to follow, your practice will be guided in a structured way specifying which scriptures to chant.

The Heart Sūtra (Prajñāpāramitāhṛdaya Sūtra)

The Bodhisattva Avalokiteśvara, who was contemplating deeply the Prajñāparamita, realized the five aggregates are empty, and was liberated from all suffering and hardship.

1. Sariputra, form is not different from emptiness, emptiness is not different from form. Form is emptiness. Emptiness is form. The same is true of feeling, perception, mental formations, and consciousness.

2. Sariputra, all phenomena are empty. They do not arise or cease, are not defiled or pure, do not increase or decrease. Thus, in emptiness, there are no forms, feelings, perceptions, mental formations, or consciousness.

3. No eye, ear, nose, tongue, body, or mind; no form, sound, smell, taste, touch or dharmas; no eye consciousness so on unto mind consciousness; no ignorance and extinction of ignorance; even unto no aging and death and no extinction of aging and death; no suffering, cause of suffering, cessation, or path; no wisdom and no attainment.

4. As there is no attainment, bodhisattvas who rely on the Prajñāparamita have neither worry nor obstruction. Without worry and obstruction, there is no fear.

5. Away from confusion and delusion, they will ultimately reach Nirvāṇa. All the Buddhas of the past, present, and future rely on the Prajñāparamita to attain anuttara-samyak-sambodhi.

6. Therefore, know that the Prajñāparamita is the great profound mantra, is the illuminating mantra, is the most supreme of all mantras, is the unequalled mantra, able to eliminate all suffering, is true and not false.

So, proclaim the "Prajñāparamita Mantra," proclaim the mantra that says: *Gate gate paragate parasamgate bodhi svaha!*

Notes

- Avalokiteśvara is the Bodhisattva of Compassion.

- Prajñāparamita he "Perfection of Wisdom". Prajñā is "Wisdom". There are several Prajñāparamita Sūtras found within Mahāyāna.

- Sariputra was a well-respected monk of the Buddha. In this Sūtra, he is being taught by the Buddha, which is why you see his name referenced (the Buddha is talking to him).

- Dharmas (with an "s") refers to all conditioned phenomena, to include those of the mind (consciousness).

- Bodhisattvas are referred to in this Sūtra because Mahāyāna is the path of the Bodhisattva, and this Sūtra gives guidance and faith to those on that path. Since all in Mahāyāna are on the Bodhisattva path generally speaking, this refers to them.

- Anuttara-samyak-sambodhi. Refers to awakening and/or Buddhahood

- The last phrase in this Sūtra can be translated as: Gone, gone, everyone gone to the other shore, awakening, hurrah! The "other shore" refers to Nirvāṇa.

The Discourse on the Blessings (Maṅgala Sutta)

A deity visited the Buddha one night in Jeta's Grove, near Savatthi. He addressed the Buddha: "Many gods, deities, and men have thought about the greatest blessings which bring about a peaceful and happy life. Please, Tathāgata (Buddha), will you teach us?"

The Buddha replied:

- "To not associate with those who are foolish in thought, word, and deed, but to associate with the wise, and to honor those who are worthy of honor - this is the greatest blessing.

- "To live in a good place, to have performed good deeds and meritorious actions, and to set oneself on the right path towards morality, faith, and generosity - this is the greatest blessing.

- "To learn, grow, and be skillful in a craft where no living being is injured and no unwholesome things are done, to practice the precepts, and to be skillful in good speech where your thoughts are filled with loving-kindness - this is the greatest blessing.

- "To support your parents, to cherish and support your family, and to be engaged in a peaceful and wholesome occupation - this is the greatest blessing.

- "To be generous, to live honestly, to support your relatives and friends, and to have actions that are blameless - this is the greatest blessing.

- "To avoid unwholesome actions, do not ingest intoxicating drinks and drugs, and be diligent doing wholesome things - this is the greatest blessing.

- "To be respectful, humble, polite, and grateful with others, be content with a simple life, and to not miss an occasion to listen to and learn the Dharma - this is the greatest blessing.

- "To be patient and open to change, to have regular contact with monastics, and to participate in discussing the Dharma - this is the greatest blessing.

- "To have self-restraint against greed and anger, live a spiritual life, and have insight into the Four Noble Truths that lead towards the realization of Nirvāṇa - this is the greatest blessing.

- "To have a mind of an enlightened being that is does not troubled by the conditions of this life and world, from sorrow they are now freed, from defilements they are now cleansed, from fear they are now liberated - this is the greatest blessing.

- "For one who has accomplished this, they remain unvanquished anywhere they go, always safe and happy. These are the greatest blessings."

The Loving Kindness Sermon
(Karaṇīyamettā Sutta)

This is what should be done by one who is skilled in good and wishes to attain the peace of Nirvāṇa:

- Let them practice being humble, upright, and capable of using loving speech.

- They will know the path of living simply, with senses peaceful and calm, being wise and skillful, and not being carried away with emotions or desire. This is how they should contemplate:

  1. May all living beings be safe and happy, with peace, love, and joy in their heart and mind.

  2. May all living beings live peacefully and safely, whether they are strong or weak, small or big, seen or not seen, near or far, born or yet to be born. May they all dwell in perfect tranquility.

  3. Let no one harm another. Let no one, out of anger or aversion, wish to harm another. Let no one place the life of another in danger.

  4. Just as a mother loves and protects the life of her only child, we should cultivate boundless love with all sentient beings no matter where they are. Our love with be beyond obstacles, and our heart free from hatred and ill-will.

  5. Whether we are standing or walking, sitting or lying down, as long as we are awake, we should maintain this recollection in our heart. This is said to be the noblest way of living.

Now freed from delusion, greed, and sensual desires, one lives in peace with perfect understanding, and transcends birth and death.

The Diamond Sūtra (Four Line Verse Version)

1. All forms are illusory. If you see that all forms are not forms, then you see the Tathagata (the Buddha/Truth).

2. All great Bodhisattvas should develop a pure and lucid mind in this way:

   a. They should not give rise to a mind that abides in form.
   b. They should not give rise to a mind that abides in sound, smell, taste, touch, or dharmas.
   c. They should give rise to a mind that does not abide in anything.

3. If anyone should think that I (the Buddha) can be seen among forms, or that I can be sought among sounds, then that person is on the wrong path and he will not see the Tathagata.

4. All conditioned phenomena are like dreams, illusions, bubbles, and shadows. Like the impermanence of dew and lightning, one should contemplate them in this way.

Notes

- "Dharmas" are conditioned and impermanent phenomena and beings. This should not be confused with the similarly sounding and worded 'Dharma' (which has no 's' at the end of the word) which are the teachings or sermons of the Buddha.

The Fire Sermon (Ādittapariyāya Sutta)

Monks, all is burning. And what is all that is burning?

1. The eyes, ears, nose, tongue, body, and mind are burning.
2. All forms from these are burning, all consciousness from these are burning, all impression from these are burning.[12]
3. All sensations and feelings that arise as the result of these, whether pleasant or painful, or neither painful nor unpleasant, are also burning.

But it is burning with what?

1. It is burning with the fire of greed, with the fire of anger, and with the fire of delusion.
2. It is burning with birth, aging, and death, with sorrows, griefs, pains, and despairs.

Monks, a learned one who sees and understands these things becomes unaffected by the eye, ear, nose, tongue, body, and mind. They are dispassionate and unaffected regarding sensations and feelings, whether pleasant or painful, or neither painful nor unpleasant.

Being dispassionate and unaffected, they become detached; through this detachment, they are liberated (Nirvāṇa).

When they become liberated, they know they are liberated. And they know that the cycle of rebirth is ended, the spiritual life has been lived, and what must be done is done.

---

[12] Refer to page 17 for a list of sense organs and objects

The Sūtra of the Eight Realizations of Great Beings

<u>Opening</u>

For all disciples of the Buddha:

morning and night,

hold them in your mind,

and chant them often,

these eight realizations of great beings.

<u>One</u>

Realize that this world is impermanent, that nations are unsafe and unstable, that the four elements cause suffering and are empty, and that there is no self within the five skandhas; that all things that arise must change and decline, and that they are but false appearances without any stable essence; that mind is the source of evil, and that form is a congregation of wrongdoings. Contemplate all of this, and gradually you will disentangle yourself from the cycle of birth and death.

<u>Two</u>

Realize that excessive desire causes suffering. The fatigue and troubles of the cycle of birth and death arise from greed and desire. Have few desires, be receptive, and you will be content in body and mind.

<u>Three</u>

Realize that the mind is insatiable and that it constantly strives for more, thus adding to its transgressions and mistakes. The bodhisattva is not like this; he thinks often of being satisfied with what he has, and he is peaceful in poverty and upholds the Dharma. Wisdom is his only concern.

Four

Realize that laziness leads to downfall. Be diligent and break the hold of harmful fixation. Defeat the four demons and escape the prison of this dark world.

Five

Realize that ignorance gives rise to the cycle of birth and death. The bodhisattva studies widely, listens carefully and thinks often in order to increase his wisdom and develop his talents in speaking so that he is fit to teach and transform others, and show them the greatest joy.

Six

Realize that poverty and suffering leads only to more of the same. A bodhisattva is generous and equal-minded towards both friend and foe. He does not dwell on old wrongs or make new enemies.

Seven

Realize that the five desires bring nothing but trouble. Though we live in this world, we do not become stained by worldly pleasures. Instead, we think of a monk's garb, his bowl, and his chanting instruments. Having set our minds on monastic life, we uphold the way and purify ourselves. Our morality encompasses all, our compassion includes everyone.

Eight

Realize that life and death are like flickering flames, and that suffering is endless. Take the Mahāyāna Vow to befriend all things. Vow to take on the illimitable suffering of sentient beings and lead them all to ultimate bliss.

<u>Closing</u>

These eight points are the realizations of all Buddhas and bodhisattvas. With diligence they trod the way, with compassion they hone their wisdom. They board the vessel of the Dharma body, and sail to the shore of Nirvāṇa. They then return to the cycle of birth and death to help others cross to that shore. These eight points can direct us in all things, and they can show all sentient beings how to understand the sufferings of birth and death; they can help us disentangle ourselves from the five desires and turn our minds to the saintly way. If a disciple of the Buddha chants these eight points, thought by thought he will eradicate his infinite karmic debt; and he will approach the awakened state, and quickly become enlightened; then he will forever be free from the cycle of birth and death, and abide in joy forever.

Notes

- This was one of the first Buddhist Sūtras ever translated into Chinese and, according to Venerable Master Hsing Yun, is a short summary of Mahāyāna Buddhism. "Great Beings" in the title refers to Buddhas and Bodhisattvas.
- This Sūtra was related to a discussion by one of the Buddha's wisest disciples, Aniruddha, asking how laypersons and monastics should interact in this world and become enlightened.
- The first part of the Sūtra is related to the Buddha's "realization" (or analysis of the world), and the second part consists of the remaining seven teachings that show us how to live in the world.
- This Sūtra can function as a "map" and "compass" for us to navigate our world skillfully as Buddhists. While this is a Mahāyāna Sūtra, those in Theravāda may find it equally as helpful.
- According to Venerable Thich Nhat Hanh[13] it is "entirely in accord with both the Mahāyāna and Theravāda traditions."

---

[13] https://www.buddhanet.net/pdf_file/beingssutra.pdf

Step 6: Meditation or Recitation

Meditative concentration can take the form of sitting meditation, visualization, chanting, recitation, or a combination.

Meditation may also be performed while walking, sitting in a chair, or even kneeling!

While meditation may seem like "inactivity," it can be extremely physical and mentally demanding.

As a reminder, sitting meditation should be learned under the guidance of a proper teacher, such as a Buddhist monastic. A book, such as this one, can never been designed to properly teach meditation based on your body, health, etc.

If you do not have a temple nearby, refer to page 143 for some suggestions on how to proceed.

You should consult with a physician or appropriate professional prior to undertaking any physical activity, which includes sitting meditation because it can reduce circulation.

Settling the Mind and Insight

Meditation comprises two parts. One is to settle and calm the mind, known as *śamatha*. The other is to develop insight, known as *vipassanā* (revealing wisdom known as Prajñā in Mahāyāna and Paññā in Theravāda).

While there is a modern Theravāda meditation practice born out of Burma known as "vipassanā meditation", vipassanā is actually the *result* of meditation.

For beginners, calming the mind will be where most of your work will be focused on. Because our mind constantly is distracted and wants to grab your attention, settling the mind of these distracted thoughts can be challenging.

Buddhism has long described this distracted mind as a "monkey mind" because it is like a monkey swinging from branch to branch. Your mind is constantly "swinging" from one impermanent thought to the next. Your mind wants you to "grab" ahold of one of these "vines" the monkey (a "thought") is swinging to.

Your practice is not to be discouraged when random thoughts occur, but to *recognize* it occurred without judgement or attachment, and let it float away. In-fact, observing the impermanence of the thought is one way to develop insight.

As a beginner, you will often "grab onto" these "vines" and follow that thought. Do not be discouraged. Just like a beginner going to the gym, it will take some time to develop the strength and practice to settle your mind.

When the mind is settled, insight and wisdom can occur, which is the goal. Meditation is a tool to help us fundamentally (rather than intellectually) understand Buddhist teachings and concepts to become enlightened, realize Nirvāṇa, and end the cycle of rebirth.

The Five Hindrances

In Buddhism, the *Five Hindrances* are mental states that are counterproductive to achieving insight (*vipassanā*) on the path towards enlightenment and Nirvāṇa.

Imagine them like obstacles on the road while you are driving your car to a destination. Speed bumps, potholes, and maybe even a large boulder can slow or stop you completely!

They are hindrances to the stages of meditative concentration (*jhānas*) and *śamatha* (calming the mind).

These hindrances "chain" you to ignorance of the Buddha's truth and liberating path. Our goal is to "break the chains" of forced rebirth and suffering through Buddhist practices of wisdom, conduct, and meditative concentration.

The Five Hindrances are something that will be part of your practice. Because these are things *you create* (until you become enlightened and abandon them), our goal is to be mindful and recognize that they are occurring and understand *we* are the ones giving it "power." Be aware of them, but do not "grab on" to them to not give them "power."

Hindrances	Practice[14]
Sensual Desire	Try meditating on the impure, ever changing, and impermanent nature of the desire.
Ill Will	Practice loving kindness "*metta*" (see page 88), compassion, and joy.
Sloth & Torpor[15]	Try another meditative position, cold water on face, walking meditation, or just take a break.
Restlessness & Worry	Recognize and observe the emotions[16] without judgement or controlling it (*śamatha*).
Doubt & Uncertainty	Faith in the Buddha, Dharma, and Sangha. Ask questions and learn from monastics.

---

[14] These are just some general examples. Refer to a Buddhist monastic for more specific and individual guidance.

[15] "Sloth" (apathy) can refer to mental states and "torpor" (laziness) to physical states

[16] Anxiety and other conditions may be related to an undiagnosed medical condition and should be addressed by a medical professional before engaging in any meditative practices.

Posture & Body

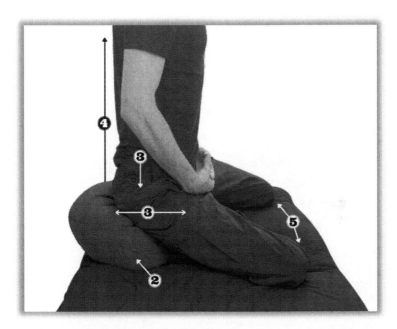

1. Find a spot where you will not be interrupted.

2. Use a sitting cushion (or a chair with your feet on the floor).

3. Rest your buttocks as far forward on the sitting cushion without falling off (the forward third of the cushion).

4. Center your spine by swaying in decreasing arcs and keep back straight (like a stack of coins).

5. Knees and buttocks are in contact with the floor. Although if this proves difficult, do not feel compelled to do so.

6. Relax every muscle in your body to include your face.

7. Slightly tuck your chin at a 45-degree angle.

8. Place a towel over your legs as blood flow may be restricted and this can keep your lower body warmer.

9. Refer to page 79 for examples of sitting positions.

Hands & Eyes

- Place your hands comfortably in your lap or on the upper foot.

- One method is to have your right-hand rest on the bottom and the left hand on top.

- Palms are upward, fingers overlapped, thumbs barely touching.

- Your eyes are open and unfocused about three feet in front of you or can be closed.

Breathing

- A basic meditation practice is to focus on the breath.

- Start by placing your tongue against roof of mouth and breathe through your nose.

- Be aware when you breathe in, and aware when you breathe out. It may be beneficial to focus on the inside of your nostrils as a point of focus. This allows you to simply observe the air going in and out.

- Count to ten. Each inhalation and exhalation are one count.

- *Note: If you cannot breathe normally through your nose, you might try using your mouth. The focus should be on your breath – however it occurs. Please consult with a medical provider to ensure this is safe for you to do so and to receive guidance on how to perform safely.*

Focus

- Random thoughts will occur. This is to be expected.

- Recognize the thought occurred and let it drift away.

- Do not analyze or pass judgement on thoughts.

- Your practice is to settle and train the mind so insight may occur.

- As you begin your practice, it will be challenging to recognize and allow random thoughts to drift away. Your practice allows you to gradually tame the mind.

Sitting Meditation Positions

The following are some sitting meditation positions that are used by Buddhists. However, they are not inclusive of all positions.

Because sitting meditation can reduce blood flow to your legs, you should consult with a professional and/or physician to ensure you are physically and medically able to do so. It is perfectly acceptable to use a chair during sitting meditation in lieu of these positions.

Lotus

Place each foot on the opposite thigh. Make sure the tips of toes are in line with outer edge of thigh.

Half Lotus

Place left foot on the opposite thigh. The right foot rests on the floor or mat.

Burmese

Same as Lotus position, however both feet and calves remain on the floor or mat.

Supported Seiza

Place a sitting cushion between the buttocks and feet. This is an easier position for taller or heavier people.

This is one of my favorite sitting positions because it works with my height.

Certain meditation cushions are made larger in size specifically for this purpose. There are also small 'benches' that support sitting in this position.

Visualization Meditation

The practice of visualization as a form of meditation can be found throughout many different traditions. Some examples of meditative visualization include:

- Visualizing a **Buddha** or **Bodhisattva** (and the qualities of an enlightened being)

- Visualizing a Buddha's **Pure Land** (such as the Western Pure Land of Amitābha)

- Visualizing **impermanence** (a modern approach could be to see the impermanence in a flower or leaf, the change from youth to old age, etc.)

For the beginner, using paintings, illustrations, or statues of a Buddha can be very helpful with your visualization practice.

Walking Meditation

Another popular practice is walking meditation. While there are several ways to do this, including elaborate and extensive efforts with special ceremonies, you will want to keep it simple for your daily practice.

With walking meditation, you are walking either in your home, or outside, in a mindful way.

By slowly and attentively walking you are mindful of your actions and connection with the elements around you leading to both the formation of calming the mind as well as possible insight.

Another method is to walk while reciting the name of a Buddha or Bodhisattva repeatedly and visualize them.

With any walking meditation, ensure you do so in a way that is safe for you while being aware of your environment and objects that you might trip on.

Buddha Name Recitation

Reciting the name of a Buddha is a popular practice with laypersons and monastics alike. This is similar in style to chanting but focuses on mindfulness of a Buddha instead of the chanting of scripture.

The Niànfó (also known as the Nenbutsu, Yeombul, or Niệm Phật) is a practice of the Pure Land teachings of Mahāyāna Buddhism and is perhaps the most common and widely practiced form of Buddha name recitation. This recitation may also be considered a form of meditative concentration by some traditions.

In Chinese Buddhism, the Pure Land and Meditation School (Chán/Zen) are combined where meditation and recitation are both practiced.

You can use Buddhist prayer beads (Mala) while reciting the Niànfó. Move one bead for each recitation (see page 136).

When reciting, take your time reciting the words clearly, and visualize/focus on Amitābha Buddha.

Focusing on a Buddha, and the qualities of a Buddha, is an important practice. This has the added benefit of helping us "see" our inner Buddha nature, and break down greed, anger, and ignorance.

Reciting a Buddha's name takes a similar structure but will be spoken differently based upon the country. "Namo" or "Namu" is translated as "Homage" (to honor, revere, respect, obedience, etc.).

- *Japanese:* **Namu Amida Butsu** (or "**Na-Man-Da-Bu.**")

- *Chinese:* **Nāmó Āmítuófó** (or just "**Āmítuófó**")

- *Vietnamese:* **Nam mô A Di Đà Phật**

- *Korean:* **Namu Amita Bul**

- *Non-Country Specific:* **Namo Amitābha Buddhāya**

When reciting Amitābha Buddha's name, you can use the *"Ten Recitation Practice"* which is perfect for a morning session, or in the evening.

1. Harmonize the recitation with your breath.
2. Complete a total of ten recitations.

Do not worry about *how* you recite, as long as you recite. This can be fast, slow, loud, or softly. Just ensure you harmonize the recitation with your breath.

In addition to Pure Land recitation practice, reciting a Buddha's name can be found elsewhere in Mahāyāna and in Theravāda Buddhism to show homage for these enlightened beings. Recite three times when paying homage.

- A general version you can use is **"Namo Buddhāya"** which is typically used for Shakyamuni (Gautama) Buddha, or all Buddhas of the past, present, and future.

- **"Namo Shakyamuni Buddha"** is also a way of reciting the Buddha's name. This is an example used in some traditions right after reciting the Triple Gem, or on its own after providing offerings.

Bodhisattvas may also be recited. For example, one of the most popular Bodhisattvas, *Avalokiteśvara* (Guānyīn, Kannon, etc.), may be recited as:

- **"Namo Guan Shi Yin Pusa"**

- Chanting format in Chinese:
  Ná Mó Dà Bēi Guān Shìyīn Pú Sà

- A more general version is: **"Namo Avalokiteśvara"** which translates to "I hail to the Bodhisattva who listens to the sound of the world."

With any of the Buddha or Bodhisattva recitations, the practice is to recite as many times as possible. Laypersons often will incorporate recitation throughout their day, not just in the morning and evening.

Step 7: Dedication of Merit

*For all sentient beings, I dedicate the meritorious actions
of this practice so they may be guided and liberated from
delusion and suffering with the light of the
Buddha's Dharma.*

Dedicating merit can be a perplexing practice to
Westerners who may consider the practice as being cultural.
However, you should consider it for a few good reasons.

You may be surprised to learn that Buddhist practice *is* a
merit generating activity. Merit is the result of good deeds, acts,
and thoughts that accumulates over time. So, Buddhist practice
comprises all three merit generating activities.

Merit is important for laypersons because it ties in with one's progress towards enlightenment. This includes future rebirths where favorable realms and conditions are ensured.

So, what is merit generation all about anyways?

- Buddhism is centered around breaking down the false concept and belief in "self". If you are doing this all for "you" to benefit, you are just reinforcing the illusion of "self," rather than breaking it down.

- Compassion and loving-kindness are central teachings and practices in Buddhism.

- When we dedicate merit, we are calling up the teaching on dependent origination by arising these wholesome qualities.

- In turn, these wholesome qualities are transforming and refreshing us with the qualities that douse the Three Fires of greed, anger, and ignorance in our thoughts, speech, and actions.

If you look at the path of the Buddha, Arhats, Bodhisattvas, and other Buddhas, they were all *generating* merit until it culminated in conditions necessary for enlightenment. So, merit generation is very much in line with Buddhist practice.

Think of merit generation as "cleaning a dirty window" until all that effort "cumulates" in a clean and perfectly clear window. Now that you are "enlightened" to what truly exists on the other side of that window, you live your life freed from wrong actions and perceptions.

So, merit generation is about consistently transforming your conduct, wisdom, and concentration through practice.

And with this generation of merit, Buddhists do something that may seem counterproductive: they dedicate or "give away" their merit which is a highly symbolic and meaningful practice.

What is Dedicating Merit?

Simply put, dedicating merit is a practice that prevents us from becoming "greedy" with the merits we generate and allows us to arise compassion and generosity in our minds.

Now, does anything "magical" happen here?

The true experience is what transforms inside of you. As you go out in the world, that firm commitment changes your actions – and actions have power. Your intention for your merits to help other sentient beings plays out in your daily actions, which in turn, can help sentient beings!

In this way, you are doing something powerful. By dedicating merit, we are arising our Buddha mind for the benefit of all beings, and not just ourselves (which would be a self-centered practice).

For Mahāyāna Buddhists in particular, this is part of Bodhicitta (awakened mind) which is important in their practice of the Bodhisattva Path.

You will also find a symbiotic relationship between laypersons and monastics with merit generation. By supporting monastics in their path, we generate good merits. In turn, monastics can accept the generosity of laypersons which helps them with merit generation, and the monastic can provide a teaching to laypersons which helps the monastic gain merits.

Do not worry about "giving all your merits away" because you have already "benefited" from its generation. Think of merit generation like driving your car to a destination. In this case, "Nirvana." The gas (or electricity) in your car continues to take you miles down the road, which is the fruit of your merits.

By dedicating merits, you are simply allowing others to be pulled in the same direction as you through your momentum. Keep it going!

How to Dedicate Merit?

When we dedicate merit with pure intentions through a prayer as shown at the beginning of this chapter, we are asking the Buddhas and Bodhisattvas to hear our dedication. If you are just saying this to yourself, then who is really listening?

The point is that we need to express this dedication *beyond* ourselves to open our mind to generosity, charity, compassion, and loving-kindness which are Buddhist values and that of an enlightened being.

While this may sound unusual, or even supernatural, in some traditions Buddhist cosmology reflects that there is much more beyond just our planet, and there are many other Buddha's (such as Amitābha and future Buddhas like Maitreya).

While this may stretch your understanding (and ability to 'prove it'), it is allowing enlightened beings to be witness and hear your dedication. Buddhist practice is *Upāya* (skillful means), and this is helps with that.

You will find that dedicating merit is often a practice at Dharma services at a temple where you can dedicate merits to others practicing with you. This can also be part of your daily practice as we are discussing in this book.

You can dedicate merit mentally, or verbally, however the latter is often most popular with laypersons. Buddhists can be as broad or specific in this merit dedication to include deceased family members, someone who is sick, all sentient beings, co-workers, or even someone who treated you badly.

You can, and should, dedicate merit throughout the day at different times. For example, doing so before meals are a common practice. So can washing the dishes, saying kind words to someone, or any other wholesome act as part of your practice.

Prayers and Wishes

A common practice is to invoke a prayer or wish either before, or after, dedication of merits. Typically, this is done before the dedication of merits and will vary depending on the tradition you ultimately will follow.

Prayer can also be included at the beginning of your Buddhist practice.

Buddhist prayer is about invoking our inner loving-kindness and compassion for other sentient beings. Depending on the prayer, it may also call out to other beings in Buddhism, such as Buddhas and Bodhisattvas, to help with your prayer.

Ultimately, the prayer is not about you, but about other sentient beings, loved ones (including the deceased), etc.

While the dedication provided at the beginning of this section can also act as a sort of prayer, you may find others you wish to incorporate. Because there are many different types of prayers, you may want to explore what's available online.

To give you an example of a simple prayer you can incorporate at the end of your practice, we can use my shortened version of the *Loving Kindness Sūtra*:

For all living beings, no matter who or what they are...

Whether they are seen or unseen.
Whether they are living near or far.
Whether they are born or unborn.
Let none deceive or despise anyone.
Let none wish harm to another, through anger or hatred.

May all beings be safe, peaceful, and happy!

This prayer can be recited either before, or after, your dedication of merits.

Other prayers and wishes can also be done during this time. For example, offering prayers and wishes to loved ones, especially those who are deceased, is very popular.

By doing this, we are practicing generosity by wishing they can hear the Buddha's Dharma and have rebirth in a realm that is conducive to liberation (enlightenment and Nirvāṇa).

For some general examples, the wish may be that they can be reborn out of whatever realm they are in now and go to Amitābha Buddha's pure land. Or it may be that they can receive your loving kindness so their karma can be burned off more quickly and experience rebirth in the human realm.

While this may seem new and unusual to you, it is a wonderful and beautiful practice to open our capability to practice generosity and loving kindness as a being striving for enlightenment.

7-Day Guided Practice

This guide has provided you the structure to conduct a generalized daily Buddhist practice.

To add variety and guidance in your practice, I created this seven-day practice which you can restart every week.

The structure is designed to follow the "Six Perfections" found in Mahāyāna but designed to be general in nature to be used regardless of Buddhist tradition.

As you go through each day, you are gaining wisdom in the Buddhist teachings, training the mind through recitation and/or meditation, and transforming your conduct through precept practice.

Note: You can use this book as designed, step-by-step, without following this guided practice.

Daily Practice Contents

- **Day 1:** Giving - *Page 93*

- **Day 2:** Morality - Page 94

- **Day 3:** Patience - *Page 95*

- **Day 4:** Diligence - *Page 95*

- **Day 5:** Meditative Concentration - *Page 96*

- **Day 6:** Wisdom - *Page 98*

- **Day 7:** Impermanence - *Page 98*

For each day, follow the daily practice steps listed previously (or the combination of them that you create for your practice.

Go to the daily guided practice in this chapter as part of a "Dharma talk" session and your "Practice" for the day.

Tip: You can add "tabs" to each day to make it easier to find as part of your daily practice. Number each tab "Day 1", "Day 2", etc. You can find sticky "tabs" online or in the office supplies section of stores.

Day 1: Giving

The Buddha said[17] that *giving* is one of the most important things someone can do. In-fact, if one knew how profound giving is, they would not eat without having given their last morsel to someone else.

Why would the Buddha say such a thing? Is giving more profound than meditation or other practices?

The Buddha was providing deep insight into the true nature of enlightened beings. True giving is the absence of selfishness, ego, greed, hatred, and ignorance. The ability to genuinely care about others over self is difficult for ordinary people since we are so in love with the idea of "self".

Buddhists who practice giving are slowly chipping away the illusion of a permanent, unchanging, and independent "self", and planting seeds of kindness and compassion in others.

Daily Practice

The practice of giving is one of the most widely practiced aspects of Buddhism by laypersons. However, it is important to understand that "giving" is not always about money or physical things.

You can say a kind word, offer support, or even give your time helping someone or volunteering at a Buddhist temple.

As you encounter others during the day, keep "giving" in your mind as you interact with them and your resulting actions.

---

[17] The Itivuttaka (§ 26)

Day 2: Morality

Morality is the only way to make you truly free.

The Five Precepts are the basic foundational rules for Buddhist laypersons to follow in their practice of morality. The precepts may appear on the surface to deal specifically with you; however, they are about *not violating others*.

When one upholds the precepts, they are not violating the life of others, the property of others, the body of others, the reputation of others, or impair your judgement so you will not violate others.

Enlightened beings do not violate others, therefore the Buddhist practice of upholding the precepts works to shape us in the same way a sculptor creates a beautiful masterpiece.

Daily Practice

Reciting the Five Precepts is the foundation of your practice every day. However, are you upholding these precepts in your daily life?

As you encounter different people and situations, ask yourself mentally if you will act in a way that upholds the precepts.

At the end of the day, recite the Five Precepts and reflect on the activities of your day. Did you uphold, or violate, any of the precepts even if "trivially"?

If you violated any, what caused you to violate it? Reflect on your actions so you can be mindful in the future. Repent upon the violation (refer to page 101).

Day 3: Patience

As we progress on the path, there will be many things that cause us to lose our patience with ourselves, others, and the Dharma itself.

Are you able to tolerate hateful insults? Can you calmly tolerate suffering? Are you able to patiently observe the Buddhadharma with care?

Whether it is an insult levied against us, physical conditions like the weather that test us, or distractions that keep us from learning and practicing the Dharma, patience is vital.

Daily Practice

During your daily activities, put on an "armor" of mindfulness to protect yourself from reacting impulsively to situations you encounter.

Using a simple practice of waiting three seconds (or more) before responding can give you the opportunity to employ patience and respond more skillfully.

For times you can wait even longer, like emails, messages, etc., you can write out your message or reply separately (to prevent accidentally sending it) and come back to it later.

After practicing patience in this way, you may find that your surge of emotion or perception has changed, and your tone can become more skillful.

Day 4: Diligence

Diligence can be found in the Eightfold Path listed as Right Effort. If we do not have the right effort, or diligence, we can face many issues.

If we rush too quickly in Buddhism to become enlightened, and fail to do so, we give up. Just like the lotus flower that grows in the muddy water, it is never clear how close they are to breaking the surface and able to bloom ("enlightenment").

Just like the old story of the "Tortoise and the Hare", it is when we are steady in our progress that we reach the finish line.

Think of driving from one part of your country to the other entirely in the darkness of night, with no streetlights. All you have is a map and the headlights of your car.

With a proper map, you will be able to make it all the way even though you can only see so many feet in front of you. Buddhist practice is the same way using the Buddha's teachings.

Daily Practice

Continuing your daily practice is diligence!

But you may not always feel like you are progressing, and begin to doubt your practice, and not put in enough consistent effort.

If you have been tracking your daily practice with an app or journal, look at your progress. Do not be concerned with "results", but instead with your diligence in practicing.

Can you add something new to your practice? Are you ready to take the Five Precepts? Are you able to visit your temple? Can you incorporate observance days (see page 106)?

Day 5: Meditative Concentration

Meditation is one of the central practices in Buddhism, although it may be practiced in different ways.

Yet, its purpose was illustrated clearly by the Buddha who used it to develop insight (Prajñā Wisdom) into the true nature of our existence. With this, he was able to become enlightened through understanding "dependent origination" which taught that all things arise and fall due to causes and conditions, all things are impermanent, and that all things are interdependent.

Through meditation, we can not only settle the mind as our first step, but then to develop insight as the Buddha and his enlightened followers did.

This is a challenging and lengthy process that is not mastered in days or years, but through continuous practice.

Daily Practice

Imagine a dirty window that is preventing you from seeing what truly is happening outside. You are assuming what the shadows you see are, and the sounds you hear.

Meditation helps you begin to clean that window. Calming meditation is your first step to "bring your hand with the brush" to the window. Otherwise, your mind wants to distract you from even wanting to clean it.

Next, after calming the mind, you focus on developing insight, typically on Buddhists concepts, or even a sūtra. This is the effort you are using to "brush away the dirt" on the window. And this will take continuous time and effort. If you are not consistent, new dirt will begin to appear on the window.

Day 6: Wisdom

Prajñā is a series of direct realizations of wisdom. Wisdom is important because that is what helps us understand that our world, and actions, are a delusion of our own making. When we understand this, the charade is over, and we can act skillfully.

This is why Prajñā Wisdom is so important. By gaining this fundamental insight into the true nature of all phenomena, we can not only end the unwholesome karmic activities in our existence but burn away the unwholesome karma we have been accumulating. This form of Prajñā Wisdom that burns away unwholesome karma is the Prajñā of Buddhas, which is why that path is sought by Mahāyānists.

However, wisdom is vital to both branches of Buddhism. Wisdom, which is a category of the Eightfold Path, helps us not just "learn" but also "act" in a skillful way. Without it, our meditative concentration, morality, and conduct will be out of balance.

Daily Practice

Wisdom is gained many ways, and the Buddhist path is how we obtain it.

Reading sūtras, and commentaries about them by monastics, can help us with an intellectual understanding and help us wish wisdom. Pick a sūtra, or a commentary by a monastic, to help understand a teaching deeper.

Have you been meditating? You can focus on a concept, such as emptiness, as part of your meditation. Use this day to focus on a concept after reading a sūtra and commentary about it.

Day 7: Impermanence

The Buddha said that all that is impermanent is Dukkha ("suffering"). He was talking about the cycle of rebirth and the impermanent arising of existences, such as you and me.

But impermanence is also something Buddhists find joyful because without it, things such as Dukkha would not have an end. It is with Impermanence we can find the freedom and liberation of Nirvāṇa.

Impermanence can be viewed by those new to Buddhism as a scary and uncomfortable thing. If all phenomena are impermanent and ever changing, that can make the ground under our feet feel very unstable. Yet, that ground under our feet is an illusion made of our own mind believing what is impermanent is permanent. In turn, it causes us to have beliefs and attachments to hold on to that idea of 'permanence' and that results in the Three Poisons and our Karmic actions.

The Buddha taught[18] that when you realize your natural state of Nirvāṇa, the concepts of birth and death are seen as what they truly are: a creation of our own mind. Nothing is born from nothing, and nothing dies and fades away into nothing.

Daily Practice

Impermanence is all around us, and in you, yet it is sometimes subtle, other times right in your face. Use nature to explore impermanence by looking at a tree that may be losing its leaves only to return later. Or, by watching the clouds come and go in different shapes. The cloud is a temporary existence, but its components have not gone away. The tree's leaves are temporary, but a new existence comes later that looks the same but is not the same leaf. Meditate upon the impermanence in you and others.

---

[18] Ekottara Agama 18

Appendix A: Repentance

The practice of repentance is something that is found throughout Buddhism, and an important part of Buddhist practice.

But why? Is this something like other religions where you repent to a supernatural being for forgiveness?

In Buddhism, repentance is a religious practice where we recognize our mistakes, correct them, and work on *changing* our mind and behaviors so that we will not repeat the transgression again[19].

Buddhist practice is aimed at helping us uncover our true nature, Nirvāṇa, which is free of the Three Fires of greed, anger, and ignorance. But because we still consumed with the Three Fires, we continue to violate the precepts even at levels we do not fully understand.

---

[19] It's important to note we are discussing the Buddhist religious practice here, not any sort of laws in your country and your responsibility to adhere to them. Refer to a legal professional should you have any questions.

These transgressions have occurred long before our current existence, and we have become the recipient of the karmic seeds created from those past actions.

And in our current existence, we create the karmic seeds that continues on to another existence. The "future" is caused by our "present" actions.

This cycle needs to stop, which is what the Buddha taught.

Why Repentance?

Without reflecting on what we have done, recognizing its impact on us and others, and why we did it, we will not only feed our "ego," but also stunt our spiritual growth.

According to the Venerable Master Hsing Yun, the *"Five Part Vinaya"* records the Buddha as saying:

> *In the practice of my Dharma, recognition of transgressions and repentance of them will lead to an increase in goodness.*

This is not only reassuring that the Buddha specifically addressed repentance, but also very illuminating.

Here the Buddha is saying that *recognizing* our transgressions and then *repenting* upon then leads to an increase in goodness.

Goodness is fundamentally part of the morality and conduct portion of the Eightfold Path for those on the path towards enlightenment.

So, by repenting we can address the unwholesome karmic impact upon ourselves due to the transgression and have a subsequent benefit of increasing our goodness.

However, this does not lessen the fruition and result of the karmic impact. For example, if the transgression also violates a law in your society, the karmic repercussions can be felt through the results of the justice system.

For the Buddhist context, we understand that karma can never be eliminated, but we have control of what we do with our actions moving forward.

We are all subject to the effects of past karma. They are like seeds waiting to bloom under the right conditions, and we must be aware of that.

However, we can *repent* and *change* our *future* actions from unwholesome to wholesome. This practice works to mitigate any existing unwholesome karmic seeds ever blooming if they find the right conditions.

This is the practice of Buddhists everywhere. We are not perfect due to ignorance of the Dharma, but the more we align and follow the Buddha's path, we can progress towards enlightenment and ending rebirth.

Or for Mahāyānists, they can be on the path of the Bodhisattva towards full Buddhahood.

How to Repent

There is not one single way to repent, and the different Buddhist traditions and Buddhist scriptures give many examples.

This Buddhist religious practice is not meant to offer you "salvation" or "forgiveness", but instead for you to be able to ultimately correct your mind (and thinking) so you will not repeat the transgression.

One of the Buddha's steps on the Eightfold Path is "Right Thought", and when one can understand how their actions correspond to their thoughts, they can prevent these transgressions of the precepts in the future.

- **Offerings:** We begin by providing offerings to the Triple Gem. You can follow the examples given for offerings earlier in this book.

- **Confession:** Sincerely confess your transgressions before the Triple Gem (typically before a statue of a Buddha or Bodhisattva) and vow not to repeat it.

- **Contemplation:** By deeply contemplating upon the transgression, you can better understand why it occurred in the first place and ways to prevent it from happening again. Are there Buddhist teachings you can use to apply to your understanding of why it occurred?

There are additional ways to repent which can be tradition specific, or simply added on to the above to deepen your practice and understanding.

- **88 Buddhas Repentance Ceremony:** Popular in traditions such as Chinese Buddhism, practitioners chant the name of the 88 Buddhas of our world. This allows us to repent, pay respect to these Buddhas, realize the Buddha nature within us, and to transform our karma.

- **Meditation:** Through meditation you can develop insight into the truth the Buddha taught, and the various concepts such as impermanence, dependent origination, and karma. This can help with transforming your thinking, so it aligns with "right thought" ensuring transgressions don't occur again.

- **Chanting:** The practice of chanting a sūtra can plant many seeds into your consciousness that help with preventing future transgressions. Or, the chanting of a Buddha's or Bodhisattva's name, and visualizing their qualities, can help transform your thinking, morality, and conduct, to be more in line with the Five Precepts.

Appendix B: Observance Days

The practice of *"uposatha"* or *"upavasatha,"* commonly referred to as "observance days", is found throughout the many traditions of Buddhism as a way for laypersons to deepen their faith and effort on the Buddhist path.

During these times, laypersons undertake additional vows and responsibilities. Typically, this means undertaking the *Eight Precepts*, vegetarian meals, and/or additional vows. These are ways of purifying yourself with a wholesome practice, advancing your progress on the Buddhist path, and developing morality, conduct, concentration, and wisdom.

However, do not think of it as some sort of magical cure-all. Instead, it is one of the many Buddhist practices aimed at helping you transform greed, anger, and ignorance into wisdom, morality, and concentration that leads to Nirvāṇa.

These observance days can be likened to going to the gym. Your everyday life consists of "exercise," such as walking, but only when you go to the gym do you begin to develop your body. The same holds true in Buddhism.

Observance Days Calendar

There are variations between the traditions and countries on what days of the month are considered observance days.

To help you start and observance day practice, consider practicing on the full and new moons (twice a month). Mark them on this calendar to remind if you would like. As you progress, add in additional days with the quarter moons.

If it is not practical for you to follow the lunar calendar schedule based on your life and commitments (such as work), you can adjust and pick days that work for you. Using the calendar provided here, pick the days you want to observe that work with your schedule. Start with one or two days and work your way up (or just stick with two days).

If you would like to adjust *what* you do on specific days, use abbreviations such as 8P (Eight Precepts), VG (Vegetarian Meals), FS (Fasting), BP (Bodhisattva Precepts), etc.

Sat	Sun	Mon	Tue	Wed	Thu	Fri
Sat	Sun	Mon	Tue	Wed	Thu	Fri
Sat	Sun	Mon	Tue	Wed	Thu	Fri
Sat	Sun	Mon	Tue	Wed	Thu	Fri

The Eight Precepts

Laypersons often strive to observe the *Eight Precepts* during these observance days as they are mirroring a condensed version of the hundreds of precepts a monastic adheres to.

In addition to the Five Precepts, the additional three precepts include no food after the solar noon ("mid-day" or afternoon), no perfume or jewelry and "entertainment" (such as singing, watching shows, dancing, listening to music, etc.), and no sleeping on high/luxurious beds.

An example of a vow you can make before observing the eight precepts is as follows:

"I undertake to observe in harmony during this day and this night these eight precepts that have been designed by the wisdom of the Buddha."

The eight precepts, and vows one takes, are as follows:

1. I undertake [to observe] the rule of **abstinence from taking life**

2. I undertake [to observe] the rule of **abstinence from taking what is not given**

3. I undertake [to observe] the rule of **abstinence from unchastity**

4. I undertake [to observe] the rule of **abstinence from false speech**

5. I undertake [to observe] the rule of **abstinence from intoxicants which cause a careless frame of mind**

6. I undertake [to observe] the rule of **abstinence from taking food at the wrong time**

7. I undertake [to observe] the rule of **abstinence from dancing, music, visiting shows, flowers, make-up, the wearing of ornaments and decorations**

8. I undertake [to observe] the rule of **abstinence from a tall, high sleeping place.**

When you practice depends on your tradition and Buddhist calendar being observed.

However, you can take a simplified approach if you are currently without a tradition you are following:

- Undertake an observance day when you can devote yourself to it. This can be during your weekend, such as on Sunday, or your day off work.

- Observance days are also linked with the lunar cycle and lunar month. You can observe during the full and new moons. Or you can decide to observe during each cycle of the moon (new, full, and the quarter moons).

Which schedule and frequency should you choose? Try them and see what best fits your practice.

While I like the idea of devoting a weekend day to this practice, following the lunar cycle is something I find more appealing since I am observing with other Buddhists around the world.

Vegetarian Meals

In everyday life, Buddhists may not always be fasting, but might restrict their diet.

This practice varies by country and tradition but is always typically aligned with not eating meat or doing so in a way that minimizes suffering.

Some practitioners choose to eat only vegetarian meals during observance days. This may be more of a frequent occurrence in countries like China and Taiwan.

Strong smelling foods, such as garlic and onion, may also be avoided by Buddhists in East-Asian countries based in part from teachings from the *Brahmajāla Sūtra (Brahmā's Net Sūtra).*

Fasting

Popular in East Asian Buddhism, practitioners fast on the first-quarter moon, full moon, last-quarter moon, and new moon which typically correspond to the 8th, 14th, 15th, 23rd, 29th, and 30th days of the Chinese lunar month/calendar.

Depending on the practitioner and their schedule, some may modify their fasting days to twice a month near the full and new moons, or more simply, on a Sunday.

But, why fasting? Fasting is not a practice in Buddhism alone as many religions also have fasting. By fasting, one is shifting their body from the constant drive to eat, and instead focus on a religious practice. As the body transforms during fasting, some believe that it helps with different practices and realizations.

Additionally, fasting in Buddhism helps us mirror what Siddhartha Gautama did while meditating before he became the

Buddha, and to help us find the "middle way" of not going to extremes - in this case, by overindulgence in food and flavors.

So, should you fast? This is a personal decision, but it may be something you wish to explore as you deepen your Buddhist religious practice.

What does fasting involve? This will vary greatly by tradition and country, however, in general, it means to eat just one meal that day, such as a vegetarian meal (no meat – refer to the Eight Precepts), before the solar noon.

It is important to stress that fasting should never be done if there are medical concerns or other reasons to avoid it. Even if you don't have a medical condition, you should consult a professional, such as your physician, before you begin fasting to ensure you will not have any unforeseen complications.

Children do not engage in fasting.

Those who take more extended versions of fasting, which may include monastics, often do so under supervision to ensure safety and correct procedure is followed.

In Mahāyāna Buddhism, those who have taken the Bodhisattva Precepts practice fasting six days a month and stop eating before the solar noon. This is done for a variety of reasons but includes the compassion of a Bodhisattva by reducing the amount of food they eat (so others who are deprived can have more food, even if symbolically).

To keep track of the lunar cycle for new and full moons, you can often find smartphone apps that help you track it. There are often online calendars that mark the new and full moons for fasting. Your temple may also have such a calendar or list available for you.

The Bodhisattva Precepts

1. Do not kill or encourage others to kill.

2. Do not steal or encourage others to steal.

3. Do not engage in licentious acts or encourage others to do so. *(Note: Monastics are expected to abstain from sexual conduct entirely)*

4. Do not use false words and speech or encourage others to do so.

5. Do not trade or sell alcoholic beverages or encourage others to do so.

6. Do not broadcast the misdeeds or faults of the Buddhist assembly, nor encourage others to do so.

7. Do not praise oneself and speak ill of others or encourage others to do so.

8. Do not be stingy or encourage others to do so.

9. Do not harbor anger or encourage others to be angry.

10. Do not speak ill of the Buddha, the Dharma, or the Sangha *(i.e., the "Triple Gem")* or encourage others to do so.

The Bodhisattva Precepts are additional Mahāyāna precepts that help the practitioner focus on liberating themselves, and other living beings, from suffering.

There are 48 minor precepts, and 10 major precepts, which should always be kept. The 10 major precepts are what most practitioners focus on.

Mahāyānists who have taken a vow to uphold the precepts aspire to always do so, rather than only on observance days.

However, they can provide an additional practice you can use during observance days if you have not yet taken the Bodhisattva Precepts and wish to start slowly in incorporating them in your practice and life.

These precepts are derived from the Brahmajāla Sūtra (Brahmā's Net Sūtra) and their purpose is to help the practitioner advance along the Bodhisattva Path.

Think of these precepts as "rules of the road" in the same way you observe the rules of the road while driving your car.

They are aiding you in correctly following the Bodhisattva path leading to the full realization of all of them when you become an enlightened being.

Appendix C: Holidays, Ceremonies, and Rituals

Buddhist holidays are numerous, and frequently part of a Buddhist laypersons experience in Buddhist majority countries.

But what about in Western countries? You can easily incorporate certain Buddhist holidays into most "Western" holidays as well. For example:

- **Bodhi Day** celebrates the Buddha's enlightenment. It is also in December, which aligns nicely with the **Christmas** season.

- **Independence Day(s)** vary by country, but you can use this as a day to celebrate **impermanence**. While not a Buddhist holiday, it can be a way for you to reflect on the impermanent nature of things.

I encourage you to participate in your local temples Buddhist and cultural holidays and ceremonies.

While some of these holidays and ceremonies will be "new" to you, you are going to benefit in these ways:

- You will be experiencing and participating in another cultures activities and understanding of Buddhism – a learning experience!

- You may learn something new about Buddhism, and a new way to understand and practice Buddhism that may be very beneficial to you.

- Remember, most of these cultures have been practicing Buddhism for centuries, so there is a reason they are structured as such.

- Yes, there can be cultural influences, but opening your mind and removing preconceptions can assist you with understanding these Buddhist ceremonies and holidays.

So, what are some "major" holidays that most Buddhists know and celebrate? There are a few!

There are many Buddhist traditions, so this does not mean all Buddhists celebrate the same exact holidays or on the same dates, but it can give you a general idea.

Buddhist New Year

Celebrated on different days depending on the country. This is not practiced on the "Western" new year (January 1st) but based on the New Year of the Asian country that is celebrating it, which is why there are different dates. Various activities occur, where laypersons will help to clean the temple, Buddha statues, make offering to their deceased ancestors, make special food for monastics, and even light lanterns.

Pavarana (End of Vassa) Kathina Ceremony

Celebrated in October. Theravāda monastics go on a three-month retreat during the rainy season (which is why it is traditionally called the "Rainy Season Retreat"). After the retreat, laypersons can practice generosity and show their support of the sangha and monastics by offering them new robes and other items they need. Often called the "Robe Offering Ceremony."

Guan Yin (Kannon) Celebration

Celebrated on the full moon of the second lunar month. Guānyīn Bodhisattva's Day of enlightenment is the sixth lunar month, and day of renunciation is on the ninth lunar month. A popular holiday in east-Asia and central-Asia, such as China, Tibet, etc., where laypersons chant/recite Guānyīn's name at temple or at home, burn incense, and reflect upon their own compassionate nature. Some may even go on pilgrimage to Mount Putuo, an island in Zhejiang Province, where the Chinese believe Guānyīn was awakened.

Ullambana, Hungry Ghosts, Bon/Ubon

Celebrated in August or September. Based upon the story, and Sūtra, of Maudgalyāyana, who was able to see his mother suffering in the afterlife due to his divine eye. The Buddha told him to make offerings to liberate his mother and others who are in the realm of hungry ghosts. There are many ways this is celebrated now where we show kindness, such as by giving offerings to monastics (bedding, daily needs, robes, etc.), providing offerings to ancestors and others, etc. In Japan, the "Bon" festival, and dance, is based upon Maudgalyāyana who was so happy that he was able to help his mother that he danced with joy.

Vesak / Wesak

Celebrated on the first full moon day in May. The most important and popular holiday in Theravāda Buddhism where the Buddha's birth, awakening (Buddhahood), and death (Parinirvāṇa), are celebrated. Laypersons often go to the temple where the raising of the Buddhist flag, singing, reciting scripture, and bringing offerings all occur. Laypersons may also release animals and insects as a symbolic act of liberation.

Dharma Day, Dhamma Day, Asanha Puja Day

Celebrated on the first full moon in July. This holiday commemorates the Buddha's first teaching at Deer Park to his five former ascetic companions. Upon hearing his Dharma talk, his five former disciples became the Buddha's first disciples and was the start of the very first Buddhist Sangha.

Buddha's Birthday

Celebrated on the first full moon day in May. Perhaps the most important and celebrated holiday in Buddhism is the Buddha's birthday, although each tradition and country may practice it differently. In Mahāyāna Buddhism, the Buddha's Birthday is celebrated separately than Vesak in Theravāda (where multiple events of the Buddha's life are recognized on the same holiday). Both the Buddha's Birthday and Vesak typically occur on the same day. Laypersons often come to the temple to clean and decorate them at this wonderful time. For Mahāyāna Buddhists, a popular tradition is to pour water that has been scented with flower petals over a "baby Buddha." This is a ritual not to "clean" the Buddha statue, but symbolically to purify our body, speech, and mind, in accordance with the Buddhist path and teachings. There are often many other activities depending on the country and tradition.

Bodhi Day

Celebrated on the eighth day of the 12th moon of the year. There are many holidays celebrating the Buddha's enlightenment, such as Vesak (which also combines other events in the Buddha's life). However, this one is specific to his enlightenment. Laypersons often use this time to meditate (just like the Buddha did to attain enlightenment), have special meals, chant, and recite Sūtras. This holiday is often either in December, or January. The December date (12/8) is often based on numerous factors when we take in our regular Gregorian calendar and has found acceptance with many Western Buddhists because it falls nicely during a traditional holiday month: December. However, it is often recognized to be in January as the correct date.

Parinirvāṇa / Nirvāṇa Day

Celebrated on either the 8th or 15th of February. Mahāyāna Buddhists observe the death of Shakyamuni Buddha and his entrance into "final" Nirvāṇa, "Parinirvāṇa", where he dies and completely escapes the cycle of birth and death. Statues and paintings showing the Buddha laying on his side, known as the "reclining Buddha," is of his Parinirvāṇa. Depending on the tradition there are different activities such as meditation, donations to support monastics, reciting the Nirvāṇa Sūtra, recounting the final days of the Buddha's life, and other spiritual activities.

Poya Days

Specific to Sri Lanka, every single full moon day (called a "Poya"), is a public holiday and day of concentrated practice. Certain Buddhist holidays, such as Vesak, are also a Poya day in Sri Lanka. Each full moon has a Poya Day, and specific name and event related to the Buddha and Buddhism. This includes the Buddha's Birthday, Buddha's Enlightenment, the Buddha's sending out of 60 disciples as missionaries, the Buddha's personal visits to Sri Lanka, when Buddhism came to Sri Lanka by Mahinda, and the first Buddhist council held after the Buddha's death.

Cultural Holidays

Buddhist Temples are part of the cultural connection of the country they are found in. During certain holidays, laypersons make their way to the temple to engage in various activities.

You will find that the temple often finds a special cultural connection with laypersons.

So, activities at a temple may not always appear "Buddhist" to you, but this is due to the multifaceted role that temples play in the society and culture for hundreds of millions of Buddhists.

For example, Chinese New Year often finds laypersons heading to their temple for activities. Temples may have performances and other things for laypersons to engage in.

Can you participate? Of course! Not only is this a wonderful way to learn and appreciate other cultures, but it also develops understanding, tolerance, loving-kindness, and connection with others.

If you are ever unsure of how to participate, ask a monastic or volunteer at a temple who are often glad to help.

Appendix D: Practicing at a Buddhist Temple

An important part of Buddhist practice is attending services, classes, meditation, and other events at a temple.

The temple is the focal point of the religion where monastics can be found, and other "Dharma friends" which are laypersons just like you who are also following the path.

Attending a temple can cause some uncertainty for many who have never been to a Buddhist temple before. Yet, you will often find it a welcoming place for those who want to practice the religion with others.

Finding a temple can be as easy as an internet search[20], or perhaps you found one while traveling around your town.

If you have already identified which tradition you want to practice in, you can narrow your search down even more.

---

[20] Buddhanet's "World Buddhist Directory" may be an option for you: http://www.buddhanet.info/wbd/

Before you head over to a temple you found, here are some recommendations:

- Check out the temples website to see if they have any information about visitors. This is an excellent opportunity to contact the temple beforehand so you can ask if a volunteer can meet you and help you understand the temple, tradition, practice, etc., to see if it is where you want to join.

- When greeting other laypersons, and especially monastics, your hands are joined together and placed at the center of the chest (often with a bow). This is a gesture of respect and kindness. However, every tradition has diverse ways this may be done so it is best to ask if you are already talking with someone.

- Depending on the temple and layout, you might need to take off your shoes which is common in many Asian cultures. However, one thing you should do is always dress appropriately as this is a religious site. This means no revealing clothing, taking off hats and sunglasses, etc. Also, do not point, take pictures, touch things, eat food or drink, etc., unless you have been told otherwise.

- Special clothing might be worn during services, depending on the tradition. For example, those who have taken the Triple Gem or taken the additional Five Precepts, may have special robes to wear identifying them as such. These are not the same as what monastics wear but are a specific style and color for laypersons.

- Larger temples may have different "rooms," to include the main shrine area, whereas smaller temples may have it all combined in one large room. In the main shrine room, you will usually see a state of the Buddha, or Buddhas, depending on tradition. This room is treated with respect, and there is often bowing before the Buddha to show respect. This is a wonderful opportunity to ask how to bow/prostrate before the Buddha in the tradition you are visiting. As you grow into your practice, the main shrine room will become a familiar and routine area you visit.

- A meditation room might be available that is dedicated to quietly meditating. While not all temples have this, you may find the main shrine room used for those purposes especially at scheduled times.

- Classes are often a staple of Buddhist temples to help new practitioners understand the religion and practice. This is an excellent opportunity to learn and grow in the religion, and often make lifelong friends in the process.

- Language may be a barrier. While more Buddhist temples have English (or your local language) translations, this is not always the case. Some temples may not have any monastics that speak English at all. Even if English is used, there will often be speaking, chanting, and reciting in the language from which that tradition of Buddhist comes from. If translation is not available, you can still participate. For example, if chanting is done in another language such as Chinese or Thai and you have a liturgy where the English letters and pronunciation goes with it, try it out. This is not only very common but chanting and reciting in the native language can often be faster, easier, and melodic, compared to English.

The most important thing to understand about practicing at a Buddhist temple is to do it! **Practicing at a temple is often straightforward where you follow their liturgy and practices.**

While not everyone has a temple close to them, you can still participate and support them if online services are available. Planning a short vacation trip to a temple is also a very popular activity.

By going to a temple, and participating, you learn the etiquette, practices, customs, and routines that you can take back to your daily Buddhist practice.

Appendix E: Practicing While Traveling

When traveling, Buddhist practice may be something you are forgetting to pack along in your suitcase!

As Buddhists, our practice doesn't begin and end only at home. Instead, we take our practice out in the world every single day. So, why would travelling or going on vacation be any different?

However, this does not mean your vacation will be consumed with multiple hours of meditation, elaborate practices, and bringing a statue of the Buddha with you.

With a little planning, your Buddhist practice can be easily modified so it takes up little space or time.

Why Practice When Traveling?

Travelling can have a mixture of extremes. From the blissful enjoyment of relaxing at a tropical paradise, to the frustrations of flight delays and lost luggage.

Keeping up your Buddhist practice while traveling allows you to "center" yourself at least once daily.

You will be reminded of the impermanence of things, your efforts to stop greed, anger, and ignorance, and to be mindful in all situations.

The main reason to practice is because your effort and determination in Buddhism does not take a "vacation".

Just like people you see working out in a hotel gym or taking a run in the morning, they continue their physical fitness practice. In the same way, you should continue your Buddhist practice.

What to Bring

Your "travel kit" does not have to be large, expensive, or elaborate. It should be tailored to your Buddhist tradition.

For example, my travel kit includes the following:

- A small version of a Mala (refer to page 136)
- An image of Amitābha Buddha and Guānyīn.
- A collapsible stand (used for smartphones, but repurposed to hold up an image of a Buddha or an eReader)
- An eBook reader
- A small, zippered bag to store these items

What should you bring? It depends on your tradition and to what degree you wish to practice when travelling.

There are plenty of custom-made mini travel altars (little collapsible objects that contain an image of the Buddha), travel incense, etc. All of this is not necessary unless you wish to use such instruments.

I highly recommend using what you have when travelling, and that is typically your smartphone.

Your smartphone can encompass many items such as keeping a picture of a Buddha or Bodhisattva in your photos app library (pin it or keep it in a dedicated folder), text of a sūtra you wish to recite (this can be in your notes app, saved as a PDF file, or even as an image in your photos app), etc. Be sure to use your phone's "do not disturb" mode when practicing.

Depending on your practice, you could use dedicated apps for this purpose. While they vary based on tradition, you can typically find apps that contain chanting, sūtras, etc., to help you complete your daily practice while traveling or at home.

Travel Practice

So, what does this "travel practice" consist of? Well, that is entirely up to you and how much time you have.

I recommend a straightforward practice that will take about five minutes in length:

1. Bow three times before an image of the Buddha.
2. Provide offerings, if desired. A simple way to do this is using a glass or cup in a hotel room and use water as an offering.
3. Take refuge in the Triple Gem.
4. Chant a short sūtra, such as the Heart Sūtra (refer to page 53) or recite a Buddha's name (refer to page 82). This is great step to do if there are disruptions like a flight delay.
5. Dedicate merits of practice.

And that is it! There is no need for a long daily practice. If you wish to add in a meditation session, feel free to do so.

Appendix F: Practicing in Everyday Life

Throughout this book, your practice has likely been in a certain location within your home.

Buddhism, however, is meant to be taken out into the world, and not just confined to a small section of your home and at certain times.

When practicing at home, you are "working out" to prepare to practice Buddhism "in the world."

You are also practicing at home to "reflect" upon how you interacted with the world so you can develop the wisdom, morality, and concentration for next time.

Generosity is Your Dharma Friend

I always like to look to the Buddha, other Buddhas, and Bodhisattvas for guidance on how to behave and interact. And one thing is consistent with all of them: *generosity*.

Generosity is something we may associate with giving money, food, or something similar. However, in the Buddhist context it encompasses everything from giving your time and attention to someone, giving your help to someone, even giving the gift of the Buddhist teachings to someone.

By practicing generosity in our everyday life, we are following in the footsteps of Buddhas and Bodhisattvas, and it is an empowering and enlightening practice all on its own.

This practice of generosity should be something you can use as your practice at any time. Hundreds of millions of Buddhists focus on generosity as their practice, and so can you.

A very common way for Buddhists to practice generosity is at their temple. They donate money and/or supplies to keep the temple in operation, food, health care for the monastics, and for various temple activities and needs.

Into the "Market"

In the tradition of the Meditation School (Zen, Chán, Thiền, Seon), there can be found the teaching of the "Ten Oxherding Pictures." These clever illustrations depict the stages a Buddhist practitioner goes through as they "tame the uncontrolled mind" (represented by an Ox or Bull in the pictures) and eventually achieve enlightenment.

The last picture, however, always inspires me. It is called "Entering the Marketplace with Helping Hands" or simply "Return to Society."

The monk - now a fully awakened being - returns to the society he left behind. He mingles and interacts with others. He can even do things that are forbidden in Buddhist precepts such as entering drinking establishments (bars)!

Why? As an enlightened being, he no longer has any delusion and can see the fundamental nature of all phenomena.

Due to this insight, he is no longer swayed and controlled by his mind as he interacts with others in these environments.

And with that liberation, he can now go where he could not go before to help all sentient beings. Essentially, he has returned to a change society – one in which he now sees for what it really is in an *enlightened* way. In return, the villagers likely see him as a changed person as well.

Buddhism is to be practiced *in the world*, not apart from it. And that interaction with others is paramount to the practice.

For example, The Buddha established alms rounds where at least once a day, monks and nuns had to interact with laypersons. This skillful practice allowed laypersons the opportunity to practice dana by giving the monastics subsistence, and the monastic could impart teachings, blessings, or other advice and teachings for the layperson. This was a beautiful symbiotic relationship that has continued for 2,600 years.

Could the Buddha have simply had a secluded retreat where his monastics could have had food made and delivered to them? Yes, absolutely, in-fact that was offered by many including kings. Yet the Buddha rejected such an extreme.

The artificial environment of their compounds may be fruitful in developing insight towards awakening, but the monastics still need the spiritual nourishment of everyday life. Separation from the world does not bring awakening, but interaction with it does which is why a monastic comes back to society.

As Buddhists we can easily be lost in our perceived goals, such as with realizing Nirvāṇa and Enlightenment, that we forget a very important fact: Nirvāṇa isn't a place separated from this world.

Impermanence and *Dependent Origination* are core Buddhist teachings. All conditioned phenomena, such as the pandemic, are impermanent. And all things arise and fall due to causes and conditions. Even though this is a very simplistic explanation of these deep Buddhist teachings which we can see them occur in the world around us. Everything is interconnected, impermanent, and ever changing - including the "world" we live in.

At various times in your life, you will be "entering a new marketplace," but is it with "helping hands" as shown in the oxherding pictures? Or as you enter this marketplace are your actions, views, and perceptions born out of the three poisons of greed, anger, and ignorance?

The *Three Fires* in our lives can be so subtle, you may not notice them when they occur, especially during times when your thoughts are consumed with doing what you want to do.

This can, however, result in the opposite of what we want as Buddhist laypersons: unskillful and unwholesome actions (Karma) that keeps us further trapped in the cycle of rebirth - *Samsara*. Why is that bad? Because Samsara *is* Dukkha for us -an unsatisfactory existence.

But what can you do? Plenty! Falling into the trap of the Three Fires is easy, which is why we practice as Buddhists. Our Buddhist practice helps us realize the causes and conditions of the Three Fires, recognize them when they occur, and prevent them from occurring in the first place.

As you venture out into the world daily, you can make the choice to interact as an unenlightened Bodhisattva.

Just like the Buddha in his past lives where he was a Bodhisattva, we can practice Buddhist ethics through morality, conduct, compassion, and loving-kindness to help others even though we have yet to achieve full awakening.

Through this practice, you can help others - and yourself - along the path towards enlightenment.

Appendix G: Creating a Home Buddhist Altar

When it comes to creating your practice area, there is no one recommendation. Each tradition can often have specific requirements on how to set up an altar, how to display the Buddha, or other details.

If you are just starting out, and do not follow a particular tradition yet, my recommendation is to "take it easy".

It can be tempting to buy all the fancy "authentic" Buddhist altars, statues, and other accessories that come along with it. *None of that is doctrinally necessary.* Yet, it may be part of the tradition that you follow which provides a consistent "anchor" and "safe place" for your daily practice.

In the following pages we will go through creating a home Buddhist altar.

As a reminder, this is a general setup we will be creating, and the tradition you eventually practice in may have more specific instructions on what constitutes an altar.

Location

If you have an extra room, or a quiet place, that would be a good location for a practice area. If you don't have this, don't worry! You can also "set up" wherever you need to.

For example, you could keep your altar items in a dedicated bag or container and take them to the dining room or living room when it is unoccupied to set up for your session.

In very small locations, you might set up an altar in a bookshelf where at least one level is dedicated to the altar itself.

An important consideration is to ensure your altar location is *respectful*. You have several items, such as a statue or image of a Buddha or Bodhisattva, which are treated with respect and reverence.

If you were to place your altar in a high traffic area, one where other distractions such as a TV or computer are located, or where you might constantly disturb it by accident, then you may want to consider another location if possible.

Ideally your altar, and a statue or image of a Buddha, will be at the highest level possible in a room to show respect.

Altars

You can easily reuse what you have in your home to create a respectable altar. Sometimes, even just a nook or niche somewhere will be enough.

Remember, throughout the centuries Buddhist laypersons often had humble homes and lives and did not have fancy things.

You can also place other items on your altar. For example, pictures of deceased family members are quite common, as well as pictures of respected teachers.

There is no need to purchase any special altar items unless your tradition requires it. For example, I repurposed an old coffee table and desktop organizer for my Buddhist altar.

Your altar (and accompanying items) is treated with respect. Routinely care for this area by cleaning and dusting it, replacing offerings, and in general ensure it is not messy. This is something you are looking at during practice, so it must reflect positively and not be distracting.

For a statue of a Buddha, it is appropriate to ensure it is at the highest part of your altar (and room) out of respect and reverence.

Buddha Statues

There is typically no mandate to have a statue. In-fact, a picture of the Buddha is fine to use and often very traditional in many traditions. For example, an image of Amitābha Buddha on a small banner may be typical in many traditions rather than having a physical statue.

We do not have Buddha statues or pictures in a form of devotion to the Buddha, but instead to help us with our practice. The Buddha is our teacher, so we show respect with a bow (which is customary in Asian culture). This is also a subtle way to help you break your love of self/ego, by showing gratitude and compassion.

The statue is also like a mirror showing you a reflection of your inner-Buddha. What you are looking at is a perfected (enlightened) being, which the Buddha said is within all of us.

So, as you meditate or chant and focus on the Buddha, you are observing and focusing on the qualities you wish to express as well.

Bodhisattvas such as Guānyīn (Kannon) are popular and found on Altars throughout East-Asian countries.

Some traditions forgo the Buddha altogether, such as Nichiren Buddhism, and instead use something called a Gohonzon.

Meditation Cushions

It is easy to find many types of meditation cushions and mats for sale, but should you get them? While there is no requirement for you to even use one, or to "sit like the Buddha" (known as the lotus posture), they can be helpful.

In-fact, you will often find elderly laypersons in temples sitting on chairs – which is perfectly fine.

Should you wish to get a meditation mat and cushion, there are many types out there. While cost is always a factor, a quality meditation cushion and mat should get you years of use.

You might want to explore getting a "tall" or "high" cushion (which is shown in the photo above), so you can sit more easily if you are tall and cannot easily do some of the other sitting methods (see "Supported Seiza" in Step 6 of the guide).

This 'bigger' cushion allows you to sit in the Japanese style, where you are sitting and kneeling, instead of doing some fancy and complicated leg posture which may be more difficult.

Appendix H: Using Malas

If there is one iconic item that people often identify with a Buddhist practitioner, it must be the "Mala", sometimes referred to as "Buddha Beads", or even "Buddhist Prayer Beads".

What is a Buddhist Mala?

In the simplest of terms, a Mala is a series of beads on a string that is used to help a practitioner maintain "single-mindedness" when practicing.

Typically, the practices in which a Mala is used include reciting Sūtras ("sermons", typically by the Buddha), mantras/chanting, śamatha meditation, and reciting the Buddha's name (such as Amitābha).

How Do You Use Malas?

The primary purpose of a Mala is to "count." While that sounds simplistic, it helps to keep a practitioner single-mindedly focused on the practice (such as recitation) itself rather than having to devote concentration on "numbers."

Since Buddhism is focused on the mind, Malas aid with counting to help one focus on the practice itself rather than counting.

While each tradition may have a different technique for using malas, the following can provide some guidance:

1. Hold your mala in one hand (typically the left, although the right is also used)

2. Begin by holding the largest bead (called a Buddha, Mother, or Guru bead) between your fingers.

3. Next, move to the first bead. Hold one bead between your fingers and recite a mantra or Buddha's name (such as Amitābha). Note that some traditions may hold the bead with the index finger.

4. After the recitation, use a "pinching motion," slide the bead aside and move to the next bead, holding it as you did in step 3. Repeat the recitation.

5. When you return to the large Buddha bead, you can stop.

6. If you wish to continue reciting, you can reverse direction. You never go 'past' the large bead but would reverse and go the other direction each time.

If your mala has "divider" beads, which may be smaller or ornamental in nature, you do not count them.

Some Buddhists may wear their beads on their wrist. While there are smaller "wrist" malas, they may wrap their 108-bead mala close to their wrist on the forearm. However, it is a proper practice to return your mala to a dedicated container for it, such as a pouch.

In wearing Buddhist beads, practitioners are reminding themselves to always keep up the practice or reciting and further practice Buddhism in daily life.

Storing Your Mala

When you are finished using your mala you should store it away carefully and respectfully. Malas are important religious tools in Buddhism and are treated as such.

1. First, hold both ends of the mala with the larger bead and tassel on one end.

2. Next, twist once.

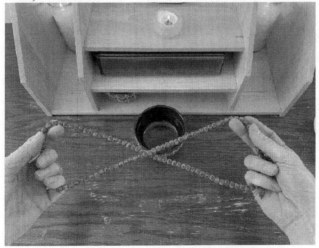

3. Fold the right side over to the left side.

4. Twist once again.

5. And bring the right side to the left side.

6. You can now store your mala nicely in a container. For example, I use a small "sauce bowl" I bought at a department store which holds a mala very nicely. You may also use a pouch or other dedicated container.

Why 108?

Ultimately, understanding what the number 108 means as it relates to a Mala will not have an overall impact on how you use it.

However, it is interesting to understand how the number 108 is so popular not only in Buddhism but elsewhere. While this list and explanation is not exhaustive, it can give you some idea about how the number 108 is important in many ways.

The number 108 is an important number not only in Buddhism but also with Hinduism and other religions (for example, in Islam 108 is used to refer to God).

Buddhism uses the number 108 in many ways:

- *108 virtues to cultivate*

- *108 defilements to avoid*

- *108 could also refer to the feelings a person has (according to some schools of Buddhism)*

- *108 questions asked by Bodhisattva Mahamati in the Lankavatara Sūtra*

- *108 temptations*

- *108 vexations*

So, 108 does have a very symbolic meaning when it comes to a Buddhist Mala!

Even if you do not have a full 108 bead Mala, you can often count "108" beads simply by going around several times. For example, I also have an 18 bead wrist Mala which can get me to 108 if I use it 6 times.

Appendix I: Dharma Services

In most Western countries, Christianity is the majority religion. It also became a way that most Buddhist traditions incorporated into the culture. For example, weekly Buddhist Dharma services are often held on a Saturday or Sunday.

There is a practical reason for this as well. While not everyone has the days off, most people have the weekend off, so it made for a good time to hold services.

If you are near a Buddhist temple, it might be beneficial to start attending services. This can be as easy as a weekly meditation session, classes, or something similar until you work your way up to a Dharma service.

Some larger temples may offer English language services and classes, whereas some smaller temples may not. This should not be a discouragement, but something to remember.

For example, depending on the ceremony, I am often reciting / chanting in Chinese (a language I am not fluent in). Thankfully, my temple offers a wireless translation and often translates the liturgy we are using or provides captions on their videos when livestreaming.

If you are not near a Buddhist temple, you can look around the internet and video streaming websites for various recorded (and live) services.

Do not be put off by the ceremony and the different practices. Most Buddhist temples are practicing the form of Buddhism native to the originating country.

Each has its own nuances and special practices which may seem unusual, but often have deep meaning and a wonderful way to learn and practice Buddhism.

My advice is to keep your mind open to it!

Your temple likely has an online calendar. But if they do not, bookmark this page and use this calendar to remind you of the days and times of services and classes.

1	2	3	4	5	6	7
8	9	10	11	12	13	14
15	16	17	18	19	20	21
22	23	24	25	26	27	28
29	30	31				

Appendix J: Dharma Friends

A journey alone is not only a lonely one, but one where your confidence and effort may be strained.

"Dharma friends" refers to others that are on the journey towards enlightenment with you. These are laypersons you find as part of your temple or group who provide community, energy, and strength for each other with their practice.

This sense of community is important because it allows us to connect with other practitioners and support each other.

Monastics assist laypersons by providing Dharma services, Dharma talks, teachings, and providing guidance. This is an important part of Buddhism because it allows us to support monastics, and for them to support us which is a merit generating activity for both.

But the ability to have Dharma friends allow us to connect on a whole other level. Since laypersons are not monastics and are mired in the everyday life of work, school, family, etc., they will have experiences that monastics do not.

These friends are like other patients at a hospital where you are all trying to recover from a sickness (in this case, Dukkha or 'suffering').

Because we see Dharma friends at different levels with some more advanced, or at the same level as you, it provides reassurance and support for questions you may have or difficulties.

If you don't have a temple nearby, it's still possible to make Dharma friends online by talking with those who are in the organization or temple you are following.

If possible, attending your organization's temple or location at least annually provides a way to find and connect with lifelong Dharma friends!

Dharma Friend Name:
_____

Contact Information:
_____

_____

Dharma Friend Name:
_____

Contact Information:
_____

_____

Dharma Friend Name:
_____

Contact Information:
_____

_____

Appendix K: Buddhist Traditions

Deciding on what branch and tradition of Buddhism to follow is an important decision.

The tradition you practice in typically has a refined and structured way to practice achieving the path in Buddhism as taught by that tradition.

If you are just starting out, it is perfectly acceptable to explore the different traditions and pick one that feels best.

Can you "jump" around traditions and "mix" them? Not necessarily. Doing so will often create confusion as the interpretation of teachings and practices can vary greatly.

What Path to Take?

There are two major "branches" of the Buddhism tree in our modern world: *Theravāda* and *Mahāyāna* Buddhism[21].

As a layperson, there is no wrong "path" to take. All schools, sects, and traditions of Buddhism believe in and follow the core teachings of the Buddha. This includes the Four Noble Truths, Noble Eightfold Path, the Buddha's Sermons (Sūtras), and teachings such as Rebirth, and Karma.

The major difference is the "path" one takes: Theravāda *(Arhat Path)* and Mahāyāna *(Bodhisattva Path)*. These are part of the "Three Vehicles" (Yānas), of which these two are the only paths in our world:

- <u>Śrāvakayāna</u>: **Arhat/Arhant** (Listeners/Disciples) - Achieves individual enlightenment & Nirvāṇa through the teachings of a Buddha (may rarely be called

---

[21] https://alanpeto.com/buddhism/understanding-mahayana-theravada/

Sāvakabuddha). Only the Theravāda school follows this path.

- Bodhisattvayāna: **Bodhisattva Path** - The path towards becoming a fully awakened Buddha to fulfill the aspiration to save all sentient beings. All the Buddhist schools follow this path (Mahāyāna) except Theravāda. Traditions include Zen (Chán, Thiền, Seon), Pure Land, Tibetan, Nichiren, etc.

Buddhist Laypersons

Laypersons in Buddhism, stemming back to the days of the Buddha, were not active practitioners like we may consider nowadays in our modern world. The goal was to become a monastic if you were really serious, and not stay in the 'householder' life.

Theravāda Buddhism generally maintains this same philosophy, however layperson practice has picked up in our modern era thanks to movements such as vipassanā meditation that was created and promoted by Burmese monks.

- Overall, the goal is to become a monastic in a future life if one cannot become one now. While laypersons can at least become "stream enterers," it is very unlikely they will become enlightened (in the classical Theravāda context).

- This is because a "householder" (layperson) typically has too many attachments to make meaningful progress compared to a monastic.

- Yet, becoming a "stream enterer" is quite a feat in itself! And even some of the Buddha's monks who didn't escape rebirth achieved this level. If this is your tradition of choice, a great guide for laypersons can be found on *accesstoinsight.com*.

Mahāyāna Buddhism was the first to push this boundary as it was focused not just on monastics, but on the laity with a path towards enlightenment while staying a householder.

- Now everyone had a direct way to practice, and the ability to actually make progress, not just monks and nuns.

- Popular traditions such as Zen (Chán, Seon, Thiền) and Pure Land grew from the Mahāyāna scriptures.

- The most popular Buddhist tradition (or practice) followed by laypersons is Pure Land Buddhism where one can chant/recite the name of Amitābha (Amida) Buddha any time, and at any place, making it a truly accessible and straightforward practice.

- In Chinese and Vietnamese Buddhism (and also Humanistic Buddhism), Pure Land and Zen (Chán/ Thiền) are often practiced together ("dual practice") so laypersons get to experience and practice these two methods.

Regardless of the Buddhist tradition you follow, this guide provides you a place to start that will be respective to the major traditions, and allow you to move to a tradition that speaks to you later on.

Your involvement in Buddhism is crucial. Our ability to even have the Buddha's teachings (Dharma), temples to go to, monastics to help us, copies of scriptures being made, etc., is all due to countless centuries of everyday laypersons supporting the Buddhist religion.

Laypersons have a special place within the Triple Gem of the Buddha, Dharma, and Sangha. Laypersons support and attend services at a temple, which generates good merits, and in-turn monastics can provide support for laypersons with teaching them. This allows monastics to *also* generate good merit and dedicate it to others.

Glossary

- **Amitābha:** The Buddha of infinite light, commonly referred to as Amitābha or Amida. Amida has a Buddha 'Pure Land' in the 'West' where anyone can more easily achieve awakening. Pure Land Buddhists recite his name (through the 'Nembustu' – Japanese, 'Niànfó' – Chinese, 'Yeombul' – Korean, and 'Niệm Phật' – Vietnamese) as the primary part of their practice.

- **Arhat:** An enlightened individual who has freed themselves from the cycle of rebirth (Saṃsāra).

- **Avalokiteśvara:** A popular Bodhisattva that encompasses the compassion of all Buddhas. Also called Guānyīn in China, and Kannon in Japan

- **Bhikkhu:** Bhikkhu (Pāli) or Bhikṣu (Sanskrit) is a mendicant and name for ordained male monks. Bhikkhunī (Pali) or Bhikṣuṇī (Sanskrit) is the term for ordained female nuns.

- **Bodhisattva:** An enlightened being who aspires to help all sentient beings, and not just themselves, to attain enlightenment and Buddhahood. They voluntarily remain in the cycle of rebirth (Saṃsāra) to help others.

- **Bodhidharma:** The patriarch of Zen/Chán Buddhism, who was a Buddhist monk that lived during the 5th or 6th century. He is credited with bringing the meditation school, known as Chán, to China. It eventually went to Japan as Zen, Korea as Seon, and Vietnam as Thiền.

- **Buddha:** The title for one who is "awake" (enlightened). We use this single name to refer to the current Buddha of our era known as Gotama/Gautama Buddha or Shakyamuni/Śākyamuni Buddha. However, the term "Buddha" is not limited to Shakyamuni. In Mahāyāna Buddhism, all beings strive towards eventually becoming a Buddha, even if that takes eons. This is different than Shakyamuni Buddha, who is known as a 'Buddha of our era.' Each era has a single Buddha whose teachings we know and follow. Mahāyāna also has other Buddhas, such as Amitābha, Medicine Buddha, etc. Both Mahāyāna and Theravāda recognize the next Buddha of our era is known as Maitreya.

- **Buddha Nature:** The teaching that all sentient beings, like humans, have the natural ability to be able to realize enlightenment.

- **Buddhism:** Buddhism is a worldwide religion with over half a billion followers, based on the insight and teachings of the founder *Shakyamuni Buddha*. The Buddha's teachings allow us to be awakened to seeing our world as it is, free of delusion, greed, and hatred. This allows us to realize enlightenment and live in our natural state of Nirvāṇa, which liberates us from creating actions, typically unskillful and unwholesome, known as Karma. This ultimately allows us to transcend the endless cycle of birth and death, known as Saṃsāra, which was caused by our actions due to constant craving and attachment.

- **Chanting:** Chanting is a popular form of practice in most forms of Buddhist traditions. Typically, a teaching of the Buddha (called a Sūtra or Sutta) is recited or chanting the name of a Buddha. Chanting is similar to meditation because it allows a concentrated effort on an object, such as the Buddha and the Buddha's qualities, which aims to transform the mind of the practitioner towards awakening.

- **Dependent Origination:** A Buddhist concept explaining conditionality. All phenomena do not exist independently of other things, do not have a separate independent self, and are not permanent. All phenomena arise and fall, dependent on causes and conditions.

- **Dharma:** The teachings or sermons of the Buddha or one of his enlightened disciples. Also called the "Buddhadharma."

- **Dharmas:** "Dharmas" are phenomena and beings. It is not to be confused with the similarly worded 'Dharma,' which are the teachings or sermons of the Buddha.

- **Dukkha:** Called "Dukkha" in Pāli and "Duḥkha" in Sanskrit. Dukkha is a term that is sometimes translated as "Suffering" or "Unsatisfactoriness." Dukkha is a result of our attachments, specifically to the erroneous belief that we (and other things) have an unchanging, independent, and permanent 'self.' Our attachments to things create actions (Karma), which result in Dukkha, which is the "sickness" we face. This sickness, which creates Karma, results in rebirth. Attachments crave "fuel," which they find with the "Three Poisons/Fires" of Ignorance/Delusions, Greed/Desire, and Aversion/Hatred. These are essentially 'wrong views' which cause us to have craving, which in turn cause us to be "attached" to Saṃsāra. Following the Noble Eightfold Path, which is likened to a "prescription" the Buddha wrote, all sentient beings like humans can heal our sickness ("Dukkha") caused by the three poisons.

- **Eightfold Path:** This core teaching of the Buddha describes the path towards awakening and enlightenment, which allows one to live in the state of Nirvāṇa.

- **Emptiness:** The concept of 'emptiness' is different in Mahāyāna Buddhism than it is in Theravāda Buddhism. Mahāyāna Buddhists believe that not only are human beings empty of an intrinsic self (such as a soul), but everything (all phenomena, which are called 'dharmas') is inherently empty of this 'independent self' or 'independent nature.' Because everything is interconnected, arises when the conditions are right (Dependent Origination), and all things ("we" / "self") are a temporary grouping due to causes and conditions and will eventually cease existing in that current form, everything is therefore 'empty' of a permanent, unchanging 'self' which does not really exist.

- **Enlightenment:** When one has eliminated all obstructions of the mind, perfected insight and wisdom, and abandoned defilements, they are liberated from the cycle of rebirth and enter the state of Nirvāṇa. While the different Buddhist traditions define enlightenment differently, Theravāda views the Arhat as the ideal. In contrast, Mahāyāna views the Bodhisattva as the ideal as they strive to become a Buddha (Bodhisattva path).

- **Five Precepts:** Abstaining from killing living beings, theft, sexual misconduct, speaking lies/falsehood, and intoxication.

- **Five Skandhas / Aggregates:** The Five Aggregates, also referred to as the Five Skandhas, refers to the temporary, ever-changing conditions that make up a sentient being, such as a human or cat. The first of the Five Aggregates, matter, is also known as "Rupa" or "Body." The other four are "Nama" or "Mind." Together, they are known as "Namarupa," which is a formation of our "store consciousness" (ālāyavijñāna), ourselves, and our environment. Sentient beings believe they have an independent and permanent self, which causes suffering (Dukkha) in their lives and the cycle of rebirth. The teaching of the Five Aggregates helps a Buddhist understand they are a temporary grouping of things that arise when the conditions are right (birth) and cease in the future (death).

- **Four Noble Truths:** The Four Noble Truths are the Buddha's explanation (as if he were a doctor) of the disease, the cause of the disease, the prognosis, and the cure for what ails all sentient beings. This "ailment" is known as Dukkha (commonly referred to as "suffering" but has a deeper meaning related to the fundamental unsatisfactoriness and painfulness of mundane life) and affects us at various times in our life.

- **Heart Sūtra:** One of the shortest and most recited scriptures in Mahāyāna Buddhism regarding the perfection of wisdom is called Prajñā Paramita. One is to take the Sūtra into the heart and uncover its true meaning through practice. Intellect, analysis, and faith alone will not be enough to understand the Sūtra.

- **Karma:** The word "Karma" means "deed" or "action" in the ancient Sanskrit language and is a core teaching in all schools of Buddhism. Karma (Kamma in Pāli) governs the concept of "cause and effect," meaning that all "intentional" actions produce results that the doer ("you") will eventually feel. Any "good deeds" would receive positive (wholesome) karmic effects, and any "bad deeds" would produce negative (unwholesome) karmic results. Karma also exists with other types of sentient beings, communities, countries, and even the earth. There are three types of Karma identified by the Buddha: Karma generated by the body (your actions), Karma caused by speech (your words), and Karma developed by the mind (your thoughts).

- **Karmic Actions:** Any actions you intentionally do with your body, speech, or mind will create karmic results.

Wholesome karmic actions are based upon generosity, compassion, kindness, sympathy, mindfulness, or wisdom. *Unwholesome* karmic actions are based upon greed, hatred, and delusion. *Neutral* (or "Ineffective") karmic actions have no impact and include unintentional activities such as sleeping, breathing, eating, unintentionally stepping on an ant, etc.

- **Mahāyāna:** One of the two major branches of Buddhism currently in practice today and has many 'sects' or traditions within it in the east-Asian countries of China, Taiwan, Japan, Korea, and Vietnam, and central-Asian countries of Tibet, Himalayas, etc. It asserts that all sentient beings, not just monastics, can realize enlightenment and eventually become a Buddha through following the Bodhisattva path.

- **Mala:** A mala is like prayer beads used in other religions. Different Buddhist traditions use them to count recitations, sūtras, chanting, or even visually to signify the abbot of a monastery. Most lay Buddhists wear a small mala on their wrist to identify themselves as Buddhist.

- **Mantra:** Usually, a sound, word, or saying that is used as a form of meditative concentration or invocation.

- **Māra:** A celestial demon that tempts humans and prevents them from becoming awakened. Māra tried to seduce Prince Siddhārtha as he meditated towards awakening. However, Siddhārtha was able to defeat Māra's actions, and he became the Buddha. Māra is also an analogy for our mind that causes delusion, hatred, and desire.

- **Metta:** Commonly referred to as "Loving Kindness" in Buddhism, it is called Maitrī (Sanskrit) / Mettā (Pāli) and is a popular form of meditation. It is also one of the Ten Pāramitās of Theravāda Buddhism.

- **Monkey Mind:** Human Buddhists often refer to "monkey mind," meaning random thoughts and actions like a monkey in the wild.

- **Nirvāṇa:** The state of being liberated and free of wrong perceptions, delusions, and their causes. Nirvāṇa (Nibbāna in Pāli) is the natural state of all beings where there is a cessation of unsatisfactory conditions and causes. However, most beings are unaware of this natural truth and are trapped in an endless cycle of rebirth.

- **Non-Self:** A central concept that states that there is no unchanging, independent, and permanent 'self,' 'soul,' or 'essence,' of any phenomena. Anātman (Sanskrit) / Anattā (Pāli). Everything is devoid of an individual self, but most beings are unaware of this truth.

- **Ox Herding Pictures:** Illustrations that help to teach Buddhists the Zen/Chán path towards enlightenment. They are also referred to as the "Ten Bulls" pictures.

- **Pali:** One of the scholarly languages used in ancient India. Most notably, it is used as the language of the Pāli Canon of the Theravāda tradition found in Southeast Asia.

- **Patriarch:** In certain Buddhist traditions, such as Zen and Chán, records of historical teachers and their lineage back to the Buddha are kept. This lineage helps to establish that a school's teachings are connected back to the Buddha himself.

- **Prajñā Paramita:** Essentially, the perfected way of seeing the true nature of reality. Prajñā=Wisdom and

Paramita=Perfection. The Prajñāpāramitā also refers to nearly 40 different sūtras in Mahāyāna Buddhism.

- **Pure Land:** In Mahāyāna Buddhism, there are numerous celestial Buddhas who have a *Pure Land* where awakening under their guidance is easily achieved. This is only a temporary place, as one will continue in the cycle of rebirth.

- **Saffron:** A color that is said to have been worn by the Buddha and other early Buddhists. It is now most predominately used for the color of the robes of Buddhist monastics of Theravāda Buddhism in Southeast Asia. Buddhist monastics of other traditions wear similarly colored robes, although not the exact same saffron color.

- **Śamatha Meditation:** Śamatha Meditation is essentially to "calm" or "settle" the mind of random thoughts.

- **Saṃsāra:** The cycle of rebirth, where birth, mundane existence, then death, are repeated endlessly and uncontrollably. This cycle is not comfortable and results in Duḥkha. One who is awakened and realizes enlightenment frees themselves from Saṃsāra and lives in their natural state of Nirvāṇa.

- **Sangha:** The community of ordained Buddhist monastics (monks and nuns). It may also be used to refer to the community of Buddhist practitioners.

- **Sanskrit:** One of the scholarly languages used in ancient India. There were numerous schools of early Buddhism, and many used this language for their scriptural canons. It is now found most notably in the Chinese Canon used by several countries and traditions in East Asian Buddhism. The Mahāyāna Sūtras found in this Canon were initially written in Sanskrit.

- **Sentient Beings:** A living being that has consciousness or sentience. Human beings are sentient beings, whereas a tree would not be.

- **Sūtra / Sutta:** A Sūtra (Sanskrit; 'Sutta' in Pāli) is a teaching/sermon of the Buddha. However, it can also be from one of his enlightened disciples or a Bodhisattva.

- **Store Consciousness:** Commonly referred to as the "seed consciousness" or "storehouse consciousness." The Buddhist term is "ālāyavijñāna" (Sanskrit). This is where karmic actions are 'stored' until the right conditions arise so they can come to fruition.

- **Suffering:** *See "Dukkha" / "Duḥkha"*

- **Theravāda:** One of the two major branches of Buddhism currently in practice today, which is the main religion and Buddhist tradition in the southeast-Asian countries of Sri Lanka, Thailand, Burma, Nepal, Cambodia, and is also part of Vietnamese Buddhism (which also incorporates Mahāyāna's Pure Land and Meditation schools). Theravāda is often differentiated in the fact that it does not recognize, or practice, any of the Mahāyāna sūtras.

- **Venerable:** Monastics (monks or nuns) are often referred to as "Venerable" in Mahāyāna Buddhism. Venerable Master is a title to the high-ranking monk in a Chán (Chinese Buddhism) or Zen (Japanese Buddhism) temple or organization.

- **Vipassanā:** Vipassanā is the *result* of meditation (*insight*); however, it is now a type of modern meditation practice. For humans, after we calm our mind (Śamatha), insight meditation (analytical) is essential to understand the world we live in and about ourselves.

- **Vultures Peak:** A famous place in Buddhist history where the Buddha taught numerous times.

- **Zen / Chán:** A tradition of Mahāyāna Buddhism practiced in several east-Asian countries, which focuses primarily on meditation. Originally from China, where it is known as Chán, thanks to the teachings of the wandering monk *Bodhidharma*. Chán has since spread to Japan (*Zen*), Korea (*Seon*), and Vietnam (*Thiền*).

Find additional glossary items on Alan's website:
https://alanpeto.com/buddhism/buddhist-glossary/

Your Notes

Use this space for any notes you would like to take as you read this book, learn from others, and engage in your practice. You will be able to look back at your notes to help plan what direction you want to learn, practice, and explore Buddhism.

_____

_____

_____

_____

_____

_____

_____

_____

_____

_____

_____

_____

_____

_____

About the Author

Alan Peto is an author and content creator who helps beginners and Westerners understand and practice Buddhism from the layperson perspective.

He is a Mahāyāna layperson in the tradition of *Humanistic Buddhism* as taught by the *Fo Guang Shan (FGS)* Buddhist Order founded by *Venerable Master Hsing Yun.*

His Dharma Temple is *Hsi Lai* located in Los Angeles County, California. He was given the Dharma name *Pu Li* during his Triple Gem refuge ceremony.

Visit Alan's Website:

https://alanpeto.com

Buddhism Articles, Graphics, Videos, Books, Podcast, and Social Media

Other Books by Alan:

The Buddhism Secrets of Cats
Buddhism in 10 Steps
Buddhismo en 10 Pasos (Spanish Edition)

Made in the USA
Middletown, DE
07 June 2024